HOLLOW**GODS**

HOLLOW**GODS**
Idolatry in a Postmodern Context

C. ERIC TURNER

Foreword by Micah Fries

RESOURCE *Publications* • Eugene, Oregon

HOLLOW GODS
Idolatry in a Postmodern Context

Copyright © 2016 C. Eric Turner. All rights reserved. Except for brief quotations in critical publications or reviews, no part of this book may be reproduced in any manner without prior written permission from the publisher. Write: Permissions, Wipf and Stock Publishers, 199 W. 8th Ave., Suite 3, Eugene, OR 97401.

Resource Publications
An Imprint of Wipf and Stock Publishers
199 W. 8th Ave., Suite 3
Eugene, OR 97401

www.wipfandstock.com

PAPERBACK ISBN: 978-1-4982-9715-8
HARDCOVER ISBN: 978-1-4982-9717-2
EBOOK ISBN: 978-1-4982-9716-5

Manufactured in the U.S.A.   12/20/16

To my wife, Stephanie. Thank you for believing in me and for walking with me on this crazy journey of life in a mixed up, messed up world.

Contents

Foreword by Micah Fries | ix

Acknowledgments | xiii

Introduction—Postmodern and Biblical Foundations of Idolatry: How Did We Get Here? | xv

1 The Postmodern Web of Knowledge | 1
2 The Postmodern Illusion of Freedom | 14
3 The Postmodern Game of Language | 31
4 The Biblical Diagnosis of the Human Heart | 46
5 The Biblical Reality of Spiritual Warfare | 60
6 The Biblical Description of a Fallen World | 74
7 Biblical Solutions for Living Faithfully in a Postmodern Context | 91

Bibliography | 101

Foreword

IN A RECENT POLITICAL campaign with a number of candidates vying for the same position, I watched as one particular candidate seemed to have a better-than-the-rest grasp of policy and governance. However, as I watched this candidate debate and engage with the other candidates, I remember telling my wife that he would never win election. In fact, my specific comment to her was, "He sounds too much like a librarian." My point was that his explanations were technical, substantive and longer than the other candidates. The other candidates seemed to have a poor grasp of policy and governance but their replies were pithy, Tweetable and popular. We live in an era where pithy statements rule substance nearly every time. We are not looking for people to move us intellectually nearly as often as we want someone who can move us emotionally. It is not the substance, but the form, that is often most appealing. Why does that matter, and what does that have to do with Hollow Gods? Let me explain.

Context is king. It is one of the first rules of hermeneutics, or biblical interpretation. The nature of the context surrounding a passage determines your interpretation of the text. Poor biblical interpretation is consistently grounded in a lack of awareness of context. Unfortunately this disregard for context can lead to misunderstood texts but, even worse, it can lead to grievous or heretical interpretations. It is a poor understanding of context, for instance, that leads us to read passages like Philippians 4:13, "I can do all things through Christ who strengthens me" and believe that it is God's way of confirming that He will help us score more touchdowns in the game, or sign more contracts in our sales career, or pass that pesky test while in high school. What we should understand about the passage is that Paul is encouraging the church to stand strong, and sharing his own story of standing faithfully for Christ, when things are good and when the bottom falls out. It is a reminder of God's ability to help us persevere in the faith, regardless of circumstance. Nonetheless, as this example illustrates, context matters.

This concept is pretty well understood across the spectrum of Christians scholars and pastors. We are quick to point out when poor biblical interpretation occurs. But while we have become adept at exegeting scripture in light of context, I wonder how effective we have become at understanding and exegeting the culture around us.

Too often, among more conservative Christians, the interpretation of culture is a negative one. We hear many constantly complain about culture, describing it in terms of a downward spiral, or an increasingly immoral environment. The problem with this understanding of culture, frankly, is that it is not a good understanding of culture. Too often we view culture in terms of moral/immoral language, which is inaccurate. Culture is neither moral nor immoral, it is, in fact, amoral. Culture has as much moral determination as Tupperware. Culture is essentially the proverbial house that we live in. It is what occurs inside the house that can prove to be both moral or immoral. Just as Tupperware is amoral, but it is possible that it could contain something that is either substantively moral, or wildly immoral, so to culture is the framework that we live within, but it does not, in and of itself, carry any moral value.

It is with that understanding in mind, then, that we recognize the need to better understand what is happening within the framework that is contemporary culture. Understanding that we cannot get away with merely ascribing moral value to culture helps us to prioritize the more difficult work of parsing what actually occurs within culture. And regardless of what culture you find yourself evaluating, it is rare, if not impossible, to ever find a culture that can be simply categorized in terms of wholly and completely good or bad, moral or immoral. The truth is much more nuanced than that. It is simplistic and sloppy to declare culture wholly good or wholly bad. It betrays a lack of inspection and care for the culture you are evaluating, all the while giving off the impression that the one making the declaration actually knows something about the culture they are describing. It is deceptive in that way. Which brings us back to the point we began with in the original paragraph.

Nuance matters for the communication of truth. We currently live in a postmodern culture. A couple of the dominant and foundational characteristics of this culture are the abandonment of belief in absolute truth (a bad element of culture) and the embrace of story or narrative as the primary means of communicating reality (a good element of culture). Too many quickly write off anyone in a postmodern culture as one who is bad, as they view the culture through the lens of its worst characteristics. It is only through the hard work of cultural exegesis that various nuanced points come to light and one is able to accurately understand those they are attempting to communicate with and, then, to communicate truth in the midst of that context.

Communication only occurs as we are able to understand nuance and context and transmit thoughts and experiences in light of those realities. One sentence can mean completely separate things based on the context that it was delivered. "Put it in the boot" can be a reference to storing something in a piece of footwear, if it was communicated in Texas or it can mean storing something in the trunk of a vehicle, if the sentence is delivered in the United Kingdom. Or consider this example. Immigration that occurs against the laws of the land, for instance, would seem fairly cut and dried. It is not moral to break the law. The interpretation of the experience could change, however, if we learned that the ones immigrating illegally did so in an attempt to save their children from extreme violence that threatened their lives. Evaluating the situation from a close enough perspective is necessary to rightly make determinations about its morality and, more specifically, to frame concepts and ideas that need to be communicated to rightly impart truth. Nuance and context are intimately vital to our understanding of the culture and our ability to rightly communicate in the contemporary context.

Foreword

It is into this word that Eric Turner writes to us about truth, its acquisition and our ability to transmit that truth to others in the midst of a postmodern world. Too often we want to ignore the culture around us, believing that all that is necessary is for us to "speak truth." We often like to use phrases like, "I just tell it like it is" in an effort to affirm our plain-speaking truth telling, but what we fail to realize is that these efforts to speak that seem simple and straightforward to us, are actually doomed to fail and miss the mark when the goal is the transmission of truth. Just because we speak something we believe to be true in a manner we believe to be simple and straightforward, does not mean it is understood that way by the hearer. I used to live in Africa, and I could preach the most eloquent gospel message, but if I did so in English, no one would understand it. I would have been guilty of misreading my context and misunderstanding my audience. I fear that many Christians today have somewhat of a grasp on biblical truth but they are misreading the culture and they are misunderstanding their audience. As a result, like me preaching to my African friends in English, they are preaching the honest truth of God's word, but they are doing so in a manner that is not understandable and no one is being transformed by this gospel.

We need to be a people who love truth and long for it. We need to understand the truth as it is contained in God's word. But we also need to do the hard work of exegeting our culture and understanding our audience. We need to make sure that our message, then, is not just preached truthfully but it is preached truthfully and clearly in light of the culture and audience. It needs to be communicated in a way that evidences study of the culture around us and comprehends the nuanced lives of the people we engage with. It is only in this way that the truth of God's word will be rightly understood by so many who are currently seduced by the Hollow Gods of this world.

Micah Fries
Senior Pastor
Brainerd Baptist Church
Chattanooga, TN

Acknowledgments

I AM INDEBTED TO Dr. Anthony Allen and the wonderful support I have received as a professor at Hannibal LaGrange University. I wrote this book with the time granted to me over summer and winter breaks from my teaching responsibilities. Their encouragement of me in this project enabled me to finish on time and with little stress.

Dr. Jeff Brown, our Dean of Students, Professor of Christian Studies and my mentor, deserves mention for putting up with me dropping into his office to read excerpts from the book. His feedback was always timely and accurate. Several of his suggested changes made their way into the final manuscript.

Charles and Joyce Turner, my mom and dad, are always an incredible rock of support for any ideas and dreams that I have sought in life. They listened and read many short stories that I wrote as a kid. I am grateful for their inspiration and time invested in me over the years.

My wife, Stephanie, has consistently offered advice and opinions along the way. Even as a busy mom and teacher, she always takes time to listen and give me perspectives on research ideas and topics. Without her and many late nights filled with coffee and editing, I am not sure the project would be what it is currently.

To my children, Cori, Chase, Carson, and Clare: thank you for allowing your dad to use stories about you in this book and also many sermon illustrations throughout the years. It is never easy being a pastor's kid, but you all have showed great strength. You all are my heroes and I treasure the gifts you are from the Lord.

Introduction

Postmodern and Biblical Foundations of Idolatry

How Did We Get Here?

A Game of Charades in a Tibetan Buddhist Temple

I DISTINCTLY REMEMBER THE choice I faced in December 2013 at the entrance to a Tibetan Buddhist temple in Southeast Asia. As part of a team whose goal was to train church leaders over the course of a few days, I found some time for examining and experiencing the local culture. Okay, to be completely honest, I was praying and looking for opportunities to share the gospel with anyone who spoke English. The chances of success diminished with each step. I truly felt like a stranger in a strange land. I could feel the spiritual darkness which surrounded me and the team that I was charged to lead. Like the Apostle Paul as he arrived in Athens, my spirit was provoked within me as I saw a city full of idols.

On this particular day, I decided to climb the steps of the local Buddhist temple. I arrived on the site expecting the Lord to powerfully work as he had done on a past trip (more on this story later). However, this event was soon to prove much different. It is customary that when one enters a Buddhist temple that they do several things: remove any hats, avoid stepping on the threshold, and walk clockwise through the interior. The temples are often manned with several Buddhist monks who seem either apathetic to the visitors or otherwise occupied in ritualistic matters. My experience, up to this point, was exactly as just described, ignorance and apathy. Just a side note, I am somewhat hard to ignore at 6 feet, 5 inches tall. Not to mention that I was one of only six white Americans in a city of 250,000 people. So, yes, we stood out to put it mildly.

My habit when I enter Tibetan Buddhist temples is simple: be quiet, respectful, and above all, pray. As I removed my St. Louis Cardinals hat and stretched one foot over the entrance to the temple, I was met with a loud voice thrown in my general direction. I looked up to see a Buddhist monk pointing at me emphatically with his bony finger. My first thought was that I had done something wrong. Did I brush the entrance to the temple with my American running shoes? Was the Buddhist monk a Chicago Cubs fan? So there I stood, one foot inside the temple and one foot outside with an agitated monk yelling at me in a language I did not speak or comprehend. That is when the game of cultural charades began. It would become a visible example for me of the choice between idolatry and faith in Jesus Christ.

I opened the charade game with a smile and a gesture of my desire to walk around the interior of the temple. The monk countered with an upheld hand and a shake of his head. I felt like I was face-to-face with the Buddhist temple traffic cop. Again, I motioned with my hand in the same manner. Then, he did something unexpected. Pointing to the incense sticks at his feet and then to the 25 foot gold statue of Buddha, he demonstrated to me exactly what he wanted. Turning and falling to his knees he bowed down to the massive golden idol at the back of the dark temple. It was clear that he desired for me to buy some incense and to imitate his worship. And, it was abundantly evident that he would not allow me to go further until I complied with his request. Here I stood, one foot in the temple and one foot outside faced with a choice, bow down to the false god before me or turn and walk away? As a follower of Jesus, the choice was easy. I shook my head 'no,' picked up my foot, and turned to walk in the opposite direction. As I walked away, the agitated chatter behind me from an offended idolater began to grow louder. I picked up my pace, urging my fellow team member to follow me quickly down the temple steps.

What if I told you that even though you reside in a Western culture, you face the same choice every single day of your life? You might say, "But I don't live around any temples that have gold idols at the center of them? And even if I did, I certainly wouldn't visit them!" Here is where the problem lies for the Christian living in a postmodern culture. The idols we have created are more perilous because they are subtle rather than overt. They are invisible masters that grip our hearts and will not let go. The problem of idolatry is not new, but postmodern culture has made it treacherous for the Christian who desires to live faithfully in its midst. Are you able to identify the idols that battle for your heart? If not, then this book is directed at you.

Face the Truth: You are an Idolater

You are an idolater. I make that statement in the most non-offensive manner possible. To be completely transparent, I am an idolater also and so is my wife, my children, my parents, my Sunday School teacher, and yes, even my pastor. You might protest, "What about the sweet elderly lady who lives next door to me who bakes me cookies every Christmas?" Yes, she is an idolater. Everyone is an idolater.

Here is where you as a reader face a choice. You can be offended and throw the book down, declaring that the author is ignorant, insensitive, and culturally intolerant. Or, you can keep reading and join me in discovering the reasons why this statement is not only true of you, but also everyone else on the planet.

The aim of this book is fairly straightforward. My goal is to offer a glimpse into the connection between postmodern culture and its rapid decline into idolatry. My plan is not to simply highlight the problem and then offer no commentary or solutions. To do so would be somewhat fatalistic, maybe even nihilistic. How truly postmodern that would be! Instead, my desire is to present the cultural and biblical reasons we are quick to follow after idols and, as a result, to provide the biblical solutions to this problem for Christian life and church health. Above all, I hope to encourage you to persevere through this ongoing temptation in your life. Idolatry is not a problem that is going away anytime soon.

Invisible Idols and Postmodern Culture

My belief is that we are quick to follow after idols. This claim may be supported through an examination of Western postmodern culture and the biblical record. Both give clear evidence that humans are and have always been idolaters.

It is arguable that our Western culture is in the midst of a precipitous fall with no end in sight. The days are approaching and may have already arrived where Christians can no longer live in relative obscurity or complacency. A shift is occurring, one that did not appear recently, but has festered in the conscience of the Western mindset. Postmodernism has opened the wound and its results are pouring out before our eyes. The change I am referencing is a rapidly growing biblical illiteracy and irrelevance married to a cultural preference for shallow, consumeristic knowledge. The result of this union is an overall decline in intellect within the culture. The creation of an intellectually shallow postmodern culture is a primary reason we are so easily led astray by false gods. Here is a key touchstone of why you are an idolater; the postmodern culture enables you not to think or consider the biblical consequences of idolatry. Why is this statement true? Because idols in our Western postmodern culture are invisible, at least to the untrained eye.

For example, think with me for a moment about the social media phenomenon of the last few years, the "selfie." Put down

Postmodern and Biblical Foundations of Idolatry

the book for a just a moment and spend a few minutes scrolling through your Instagram, Twitter, or Facebook app on your smartphone. Count the number of "selfies" on your timeline. How many did you find? As I am writing this chapter, I counted 15 on my Instagram account. Let's face the facts, we are in love with ourselves. Maybe you have only a handful of these on your social media pages. However, we all have that one friend. You know who I am referencing. I don't even have to say their name, that one friend who not only posts a "selfie," but their pages are filled with them. If you are like me, you think the same thing, "I would rather see a picture of the Grand Canyon from your vacation than your face in front of the Grand Canyon." I apologize if that was a culturally insensitive statement, but it doesn't make it any less true.

My illustration should be well-taken. While very few Christians would ever put a gold statue in their living room, offering sacrifices to it daily, we have no problem posting a picture of ourselves, checking our status updates for the number of sacrificial "likes" we receive. The worship of ourselves has subtly crept into our lives and the culture says it is perfectly normal. I am not saying it is idolatrous to post a "selfie," but only that I am encouraging you to think about why you do what you do. Is it for the approval of men? Is it so you can feel better about yourself? The idolatry perpetuated by our culture is dangerous, it is invisible. The "selfie stick" is another story altogether. Let's agree not to go there, okay?

So far I am only giving you a taste of the idolatry that postmodern culture exemplifies. In the next few chapters, I plan to further illuminate and illustrate the specific elements within our postmodern culture that cause our idols to be invisible rather than visible. These components include our postmodern views on knowledge, freedom, and language. In other words, it is critical to understand how postmodern proponents think, act, and talk.

The chapters ahead will explore why postmoderns are so skeptical about foundational objective truth, why they are enamored with the equality of outcomes for all of humanity, and why they are fascinated with how we speak about religion. These questions will form a basis for moving the conversation into the biblical reasons we fall into idolatry. Hopefully, along the way you will be able to identify the invisible idols that demand worship from you. As a result, you will become equipped as a disciple of Jesus Christ to resist and stand firm.

Visible Idols and Biblical Revelation

The Bible reveals idolatry as the result of humanity's sinfulness. In fact, the principle may be established that self-dependence and autonomy were never intended for humanity; they are the unintended consequences of the Fall, a reversal of the Garden of Eden. Therefore, it is no surprise that the biblical narrative is saturated with humanity's choice to follow after idols rather than the God who created them in his own image. One example for now will suffice to prove my point.

Exodus 32 stands as a turning point in the history of Israel. For those who are unfamiliar with the account, allow me briefly to narrate the context. God has freed the nation of Israel from 400 years of slavery through an unlikely and unwilling hero, Moses. They are led through the wilderness of Sinai to a mountain. God tells the people through his servant Moses that if they obey his voice and keep his covenant that they will be his treasured possession among all the nations of the earth. The people respond by simply saying, "All that the Lord has spoken we will do" (Exodus 19:8). As a result, Moses ascends the mountain to meet with the Lord while the people separate themselves upon fear of death.

All would be well if the story ended at this point. However, the meeting between God and Moses apparently took a long time. How long? We can only speculate. What we do know is that it was long enough for the people to ask the unthinkable of Aaron. In Exodus 32:1 we read these words,

> When the people saw that Moses delayed to come down the mountain, the people gathered themselves together to Aaron and said to him, "Up, make us gods who shall go before us. As for this Moses, the man who brought

Postmodern and Biblical Foundations of Idolatry

us up out of Egypt, we do not know what has become of him."

Two glaring problems stand out with the words of the Israelites. First, Moses was not the one who brought them out of slavery, it was God. Second, God was the one who went before them and led them. Now they are asking for false gods to lead them, a violation of the covenant they had just made with the Lord, a transgressing of the first commandment. The result of their idolatry is even more shocking. God tells Moses to go down from the mountain and observe how quickly (Exodus 32:8) his people have corrupted themselves with idols. Furthermore, God tells Moses to stand back while his wrath consumes the entire nation, "don't worry Moses, after I am done quickly laying waste to the people I just rescued, I will start over and build a new nation from you." Thankfully for the people of Israel, Moses begs God to remember his covenant with Abraham and relent from destroying Israel for the sake of his reputation. God listens.

This biblical illustration reveals for us the areas where idolatry intersects with humanity both internally and externally. I am only speculating at this point, but I am fairly confident that you did not spend the last weekend dancing around a golden calf in your backyard. However, I am certain that there was, is, or will be a time in your life where you feel that God is absent and you will look to yourself and your own wisdom and past experiences for solutions. Is that not the essence of Israel's actions at Sinai? God is busy. Moses is gone. What should we do? I know, let's build a golden calf to worship and lead us. Be sure of this my friends, the golden calf was not a new idea; they learned it in Egypt.

Are you beginning to see how dangerously subtle idolatry is? It may go something like this in your life. You are faced with a decision. Answers are not coming through prayer. You counsel with some of your friends and one of them says to you, "Just trust your heart." May I be so bold as to say that is the worst advice in the history of the universe? Idolatry begins and resides in the human heart. Our hearts produce idols faster than Apple can introduce a new version of the iPhone. In chapter four we will dig deeper into this biblical diagnosis, asking why the human heart is so quick to create, follow, and worship idols. The Bible also makes it clear that we as Christians are fighting a spiritual war with idolatry. In chapter five, we will explore why humanity is losing the idolatry war. Chapter six will address a final biblical reason that idolatry is rampant, it rests in the reality of a fallen world. This chapter will wrestle with why idolatry is prevalent, yet ignored by a majority of Christians in Western culture.

For now, you may be feeling a little hopeless or skeptical. Does a solution exist for the problem of idolatry? If everyone is an idolater and the culture is saturated with idols, should we renounce and sell all our worldly possessions and move to an organically fueled commune in Canada? Certainly not, for it is probable that we would discover idols anywhere we would choose to go. So what is the solution? Is it found in praying harder? Do I need to join a small group at church for accountability? Is this book I am reading the answer? Please allow me to offer some light on where we are going. After all is said and done, our final chapter will summarize and synthesize for you the biblical solutions for how you as a Christian can live faithfully in an idolatrous postmodern context. Yes, the answer is the Bible. But, before we arrive at the end of the matter, follow me for just a minute back to the 1980's.

The Birth of the MTV Culture: Is there a Solution to the Problem?

If you remember the 1980's, then you should clearly remember the birth of Music Television, MTV. If you are not a child of the 80's, well, I am sorry you missed out on one of the greatest decades ever. But, I digress. The MTV plan was to provide 24 hours of music videos from your favorite artists, not an endless stream of crazy reality shows as it currently stands. Very soon, what had become invisible (a voice on a radio), now became visible (a face on a screen). The results are rather comical when you observe them today. Trust me, just Google a 1980's heavy metal hair band video and you will understand. However, they were not comical to teenagers at the time that MTV arrived. We were glued to our television sets, impatiently awaiting the newest Michael Jackson video. MTV took the imagination of our own minds and injected it with visual realities which we drank down over and over again.

The existence and evolution of MTV reveals the fundamental struggle with the idols in our own heart. We idealize and yes, idolatrize the way things should be and when someone provides that very longing, a visible idol is born. We long for someone to idealize and create a perfect world for us set to the music of a beautiful god/goddess, a perfect world we believe we will find, but deep down we know does not exist.

The good news is that the answer for the problem of idolatry does not lie within the hair band ballads of the 1980's. Instead, the remedy is found in God's biblical revelation, a postmodern worldview will just not do. This statement is the path we will follow in this book. You will never find the answers to the problem of idolatry *within* the culture. You will find the solutions *apart* from culture, in the biblical revelation that God gave to us. For it is in the pages of Scripture that we discover not a god, but *the* God, the only one worthy of glory and worship, the only one who can eternally fix our idolatrous hearts.

1

The Postmodern Web of Knowledge

Defining Postmodernism: Cracker Barrel on a Saturday Night

BEFORE I BECAME A pastor and now a college professor, I worked for nine years at one of the greatest restaurants ever invented, Cracker Barrel. My time at the Barrel began with waiting tables in college at the University of Missouri, Columbia and ended in Kansas City, MO with a clear call to ministry as I left the store where I was a General Manager. I always tell the joke with a little tinge of truth that my time at Cracker Barrel prepared me for pastoring. How is that you ask? People are always hungry and grumpy which inevitably leads to conflict management. The same is true the night of a typical church business meeting, especially if the casseroles are cold and unidentifiable.

Since you have probably visited a Cracker Barrel on a Saturday night, you can relate to what I am about to describe. If not, then cancel your dinner plans for Saturday and find the nearest location. The two words which best describe the restaurant on a

Saturday night are chaos and confusion. For those unfamiliar with the way a restaurant works behind the scenes, it is a little like receiving a shot of adrenaline and then attempting to manage a crisis with limited resources and people who yell constantly. When one part of the process breaks down the dominos start to fall and the next thing you know, an employee is in the corner of the break room crying, chain smoking, and having a panic attack.

Cracker Barrel's mission statement is simple, please people. If I were to ask you to describe and define *how* a Cracker Barrel works with all of its moving parts and chaos on a Saturday night, you would struggle. You understand, however, the essence of what the restaurant is trying to do, feed people and make money. But watching it all put together, it is a little like explaining the significance of Johnny Cash to someone who hates country music.

Defining postmodernism is akin to describing a Cracker Barrel on a busy Saturday night. Just when you think you have the essence of what is going on, it changes, many times in contradictory, complex ways. Bruce Proctor affirms this struggle when he says that, "The essence of postmodernism is deconstruction without reconstruction, antithesis without synthesis."[1] For our purposes, we might offer a simple definition of postmodernism: a set of beliefs about knowledge, freedom, and language which are grounded in the rejection or modification of the modern notions of these ideas. Spend fifteen minutes talking to the barista of your local hipster coffee shop after asking him an existential question and you will scratch the surface of that definition. After all, that's how long it will take him to make your coffee. This definition will give us a way forward in the dialogue about postmodernity and its effect on the cultural reality of idolatry.

Postmodern Knowledge: Ron Swanson's Legacy

First, it is critical that we address how postmodernism affects epistemology, that is, the belief about the origins, nature, and validity

---

1. Proctor, *A Definition and Critique of Postmodernism*, 15.

The Postmodern Web of Knowledge

of knowledge. The core narrative here is found in the contributing factors for how postmodern thinkers view knowledge. As we attempt to peel back the layers on this component, the question which must be asked is, why are postmoderns so skeptical about foundational objective truth? The answer to this question is found not only in the developmental factors that have led to postmodern views on knowledge, but also the fundamental shift in Western culture towards the idolatrous worship of man. Perhaps the best way forward is to examine what postmoderns believe about the origin, nature, and validity of knowledge. But first, let's consider a recent illustration from our Western culture.

No one epitomizes postmodern skepticism more than the character Ron Swanson from the NBC show, *Parks and Recreation*. Again, if you have never seen the show, there is always Netflix or YouTube. In one telling episode, Ron gives a speech to a group of young boys on a basketball team. As their coach, he encourages them that if they follow his guidance they will grow from boys to men, from men to gladiators, and from gladiators to Swansons. In order to emphasize his point he refers to a diagram of a pyramid, a rubric for life that he has worked on for years. He refers to it as the Pyramid of Greatness and describes it as a perfectly calibrated recipe for maximum personal achievement.

The Pyramid of Greatness is nothing more than a loosely connected web of opinions with no foundation in any sort of consistent ethical norm. For example, towards the top of the pyramid two contradictory blocks sit side-by-side. One references teamwork and makes the comment, "Work together as if your life depends on it. . .IT DOES!" The block next to it simply says "Selfishness" with the by-line, "Take what is yours." We could give more examples, but you get the point. We need not take time to understand why Ron Swanson placed the avoidance of skim milk twice into the pyramid, although this is one area I happen to agree with him.

The question we posed earlier is critical, why are postmoderns so skeptical about foundational objective truth? To state the matter plainly; they do not believe that objective truth exists. Like the Swanson Pyramid of Greatness, postmoderns often piece together a web of loosely connected, contradictory thoughts into an illusion of an objective epistemological structure. While they have thought about what they believe to be true, they are not concerned with whether or not what they believe to be true is consistent. They plunge the knife into the body of knowledge available, mostly from the Internet, and truncate a consistent epistemology on the altar of cultural change. In order to understand the biblical response to the way in which postmoderns view knowledge, we turn to a deeper examination of their views on its origin, nature, and validity. If you have not already guessed, I am going to challenge you as the reader to think deeply and clearly about these concepts. Do not shy away from using your mind, lest you fall into the postmodern web of idolatry from which many do not survive.

Origins of Knowledge: iPhone or Android?

My oldest son and I often have the debate about which is better, his Samsung Android phone or my Apple iPhone. The conversation usually goes something along these lines. He says, "Dad, did you know my phone can do _____?" To which I respond, "That's nothing, did you know my iPhone can do _____?" The disagreement will never be resolved, that is, until he begins to come to the light of the supremacy of Apple and shun the Android dark side. The reason we banter about our phones is because of preference. It is subjective. The truth is that objectively, the main two operating systems are excellent. The line is crossed and problems begin when one person exalts their subjective preference as the truth. So it is with how postmoderns view the origin/basis of knowledge.

Where does knowledge originate? Whether we like it or not, the modern answer to this question is a result of the Enlightenment's optimistic view of man, that is, the view that knowledge is not innate, but a product of our experience. How does this belief translate into current postmodern culture? The deconstruction of objective ideas and values in the current postmodern culture wed

The Postmodern Web of Knowledge

to Enlightenment views on the subjective origins of knowledge has given birth to the exaltation of humans, and primarily human experience, as the source of all that is known or can be known.

Take a second a read that last sentence one more time. I warned you that you will have to think. The result of this unholy birth is that knowledge, in a postmodern system, becomes relativistic and unpredictable. If no objective source for knowledge exists outside of subjective, relativistic human experience, then the veritable ethical train will be permanently off the tracks. And, I would argue, the outcome will be an increase in the exaltation of pleasure and the worship of man. When humans become the source of knowledge, the subjective turn is always to idolatry. Consider with me for a moment about how dangerous such a subjective view on the origins of knowledge can be in our postmodern culture.

At the Christian college where I teach, we have noticed a troubling phenomenon. No, I am not talking about the rising economic costs of Netflix fees and Internet usage on campus. What I am speaking about is not our students, but their parents. It is disturbing when a parent takes their child to college, drops them off at their dorm, and then one week into the semester makes a phone call telling their fragile freshman college student that they are getting a divorce: not cool mom and dad, not cool at all. Why would something like this happen? It happens because our culture has adopted a subjective, relativistic view on the experience of marriage. If our knowledge of what it means to be married is based only on the subjective experience of being married, then it can easily be thrown aside, even when the occasion makes one scratch their head in disbelief. When the idol becomes our own feelings or experiences, we will always shun objective ethical standards. And it will not matter whether those standards are cultural or biblical.

Since the origins of knowledge played out in the relativistic, subjective realm of human experience have, we would argue, inconsistent and illegitimate results, there must be another way. The biblical view that knowledge originates with and resides in God alone is not only satisfactory, but objectively viable. It is not my intent here to offer a philosophical defense of the origins of divine knowledge, but only to present what the Bible says.[2] I will leave it up to you to decide which one provides a satisfactory and consistent answer.

Job 37:16 says that God is perfect in knowledge. Job 21:22 reminds us that no one is able to teach God anything. Ephesians 3:18–20 instructs us to comprehend what God is doing in the church in the light of the one who is able to do far more abundantly than we could think. Perhaps one of the most stinging rebukes of man's wisdom is found in 1 Corinthians 1:20–21. After speaking about the foolish message of the cross, Paul asks, "Where is the wise man? Where is the scribe? Where is the debater of this age? Has not God made foolish the wisdom of the world? For since in the wisdom of God the world through its wisdom did not come to know God, God was well-pleased through the foolishness of the message preached to save those who believe." At that point, Paul could have just dropped the mic and walked off the stage.

What is the satisfaction in locating the origins of knowledge in God and not man? The answers should be abundantly clear. God's knowledge is perfect, humanity's knowledge is imperfect. God does not need instruction in wisdom, humanity does. If you doubt such a statement, take time to read the book of Proverbs. God encourages us to strive for his knowledge, not our own. Locating the origin of knowledge in God should result in humility towards God and one another and ultimately, worship of the Creator. However, sourcing knowledge in humans results in the exaltation of man over God, the epitome of idolatry. Man's knowledge will always come up short.

---

2. This statement is not meant to imply that we can know nothing from human perception or reasoning. Certainly, we perceive or reason towards objective truths each and every day. Furthermore, I would concede that knowledge may be transmitted objectively from one person to another. What I am arguing for here is that the tendency to source knowledge in the realm of these areas alone is a dangerous practice that leads to the exclusion of the divine source of knowledge. One could argue that these areas of knowledge are dependent or subordinate to the wisdom of God. In other words, were we not made in God's image, we would not be able to empirically perceive or reason towards what is objectively true, all other things being equal.

The Postmodern Web of Knowledge

The Nature of Knowledge: Danger on the Navajo Indian Reservation

The nature of knowledge wrestles with the question of what it means for someone to know something, or not know something. In other words, we are operating in the realm of how a person knows whether or not a given propositional statement is true or false. It is critical that we move away from statements that begin with, "I know that _____." For instance, the following statement is propositionally true; I know that my heart is beating. How do I know that my heart is beating? Well, because I wrote the next sentence. Statements such as these can be misleading when it comes to understanding the nature of knowledge. The reason for this is because I can construct any statement that is true based upon my belief that it is true. But, what about statements that I believe to be true, but which are not factually true. For example, I could say, "I know that the St. Louis Cardinals are going to win the World Series this year." I believe that statement to be true, I want it to be true, but it may turn out to be false. This illustration is important for why belief is central for understanding what it means to know something.

Belief is a necessary, but not a sufficient cause of what we know. Our growth in knowledge, then, may often be measured by what we believe to be true and/or false. It is at this point that postmodern thinkers will raise their hands and wiggle in their seats, begging to ask the question; "Is truth not relative and if so, then how can one rely on belief to know anything?" A proper response might be, "If truth is localized to each individual's experiences and thereby relative, then factual knowledge is an illusion. We can never know anything that is real or that anything is real." Postmodernism relishes in this sort of exchange. However, it is a fatal blow to the human desire to know that something is or is not true. Okay, take a deep breath and let me paint an analogy for you.

Six years ago, I led a mission team of 82 people to the Navajo Indian Reservation in Arizona. Truth be told, it was technically not a mission team, but my entire congregation. The week was incredible as we labored among the churches and the people, sharing the gospel and building into the community. However, as the team began to return home, sickness struck. Team members were left behind in hospitals. As I drove our church van through Kansas, I rode through a majority of the state with my head out of the window while the rest of the van clutched their barf bags. By the way, it was the middle of July. Somehow I managed to avoid the sickness, that is, until one week after things had settled down. Sitting in my office, I began to feel strange. The left side of my face began to go numb. My mind felt like it was in a fog. I walked two blocks to our local chiropractor, a church member and deacon. Did I mention the town I pastored in did not have a Wal Mart or a hospital? After seeing Daniel, he did not mention the word stroke, but that is what I was beginning to believe was happening to me. Another one of our deacons, Roger, put me in his truck and drove me to the hospital, one hour away.

As it turned out, after an uncomfortable MRI, it was determined that I was not having a stroke. I was severely dehydrated and suffering from an infection that was common to the Navajo Reservation. I was given an IV bag of antibiotics and able to go home the next day. Here is my point. I had all the symptoms of stroke; I could not think straight, put my sentences together, and one side of my face was numb. The belief I held did not match the truth of my experience. I believed I was having a stroke. For the record, so did Daniel and Roger. Even though our beliefs were derived from the experiences of what we knew of strokes, that certainly was not the factual truth. And, as you may guess, I am grateful for the divergence between the two.

Herein lies the problem with elevating human experience(s) to the level of belief. The result could be a false proposition. When false experiences embed themselves in the realm of belief, they become difficult to unravel. Furthermore, the person who believes a proposition to be true that is inherently false often rejects attempts to otherwise learn the truth. The biblical character that fits these descriptions is Jonah. Why did Jonah get swallowed by a giant fish

The Postmodern Web of Knowledge

which ultimately vomited him on dry land? Because he believed that the city of Nineveh and its inhabitants were worthy of judgment, not mercy. Jonah knew that the Lord is a "gracious and compassionate God, slow to anger and abundant in lovingkindness, and one who relents concerning calamity."[3] Catch this important point; Jonah knew the truth about the Lord, but he did not believe it to be true of the rebellious inhabitants of Nineveh. Ironically, the experiences of his own rebellion and God's subsequent mercy on him had not affected what he believed to be true of the Ninevites. A disconnect existed between Jonah's false beliefs and the nature of knowledge.

Returning to our initial question; what does it mean to know something or not know something? We really have only two choices. Either we will locate the answers within ourselves and our experiences or outside of ourselves. To place the process of knowledge solely in human experience betrays the divine revelation that God gave to us in the Bible. Our experiences may teach us true propositions, but not always. We need an objective standard outside of ourselves, lest we are quickly led astray. My experiences and the feelings associated with them often falsely instruct me that I am the center of the universe. To make this the process by which I know truth will lead me into isolated relativism, the enthronement of my feelings as king, and the subsequent worship of self. However, by looking to God's revelation as the process by which I gain knowledge I learn truths that push back against my experiences. For instance, I might be experiencing a feeling of loneliness which leads me to the belief that I am alone. Nevertheless, when I ground my knowledge in God's word, I discover a different truth. Psalm 139 instructs me that there is nowhere in the universe I can flee from the presence of God. Learn this truth well my friend: your feelings, left unchecked by God's word, will turn your heart into an idol factory. What does it mean to know something, or not know something? While God's word is not the sum total of all *possible* knowledge, it must be the foundation and the check for objective knowledge and the avoidance of raising our feelings up as an idol.

3. Jonah 4:2.

The Validity of Knowledge: Blank Final Exams

I am a college professor, so the validity of knowledge is very important to what I do each and every day. If knowledge is relative and holds validity only in the eyes of each individual person, then I might as well stop giving lectures and certainly, final exams. In fact, denying the validity of knowledge is ridiculous in practice on a college campus. It would be like me teaching passionately on a subject all semester and then, come final exam time, handing out a blank sheet of paper with the instructions, "Just write what you feel to be true about the class." For my students reading this chapter, lest you get excited, the chances of that happening are about the same as Miley Cyrus doing a guest lecture on modesty at a Southern Baptist Seminary; not going to happen.

Denying the existence of a valid, objective standard for knowledge is problematic not only for teaching, but also for life in general. Some postmoderns would stop me at this point and protest that a difference exists between *science* and *morality*. In other words, objective knowledge is acceptable in the scientific realm because we can measure and explain the evidence. But, in the realm of morality, culture subjectively determines the standard of what we know is true. What should we say?

C. S. Lewis would argue that even though cultures appropriate morality differently, that does not mean that no objective standard of morality exists.[4] No one that I know of would argue that what ISIS is doing in the Middle East is valid because after all, morality is relative to culture and *their* culture teaches the acceptance of brutal beheadings, systematic torture, rape, and complete destruction of their enemies. I think even the most postmodern thinker would recoil from such horror, yet in the same breath explain away the brutal genocide of 60 million human beings through the culturally acceptable practice of abortion. When morality is left to be applied in a relative, subjective manner, the result is not only inconsistency, but hypocrisy. Whether we like it or not, our hearts long for equitable justice applied from an objective moral standard.

---

4. Lewis, *Mere Christianity*, 11.

The Postmodern Web of Knowledge

One of my favorite passages in the Old Testament is Isaiah 55:8–11. It is worth quoting at length here and relating it to our conversation on the validity of knowledge. To those who rely on and trust in culture and its idols for the validity of knowledge, you would do well to hear the warning God gives to his people who, by the way, consistently followed idols.

> "For My thoughts are not your thoughts, Nor are your ways My ways," declares the Lord. "For as the heavens are higher than the earth, So are My ways higher than your ways, And My thoughts than your thoughts."

I hope you get the connection I am making for you. The ways of humanity will always come up short in the domain of objective knowledge, especially as it relates to the understanding of the divine providence of God. You have a choice to make Christian. Will you look to the culture for the validity of knowledge? Or, will you look to God? The former will lead you to the potter's wheel where you will construct an empty, hollow god that can never deliver you. The latter will lead you to the God who created and formed you to know Him. The reason you and I are so quick to create our own truth and declare it valid resides in a rebellious, sinful nature that refuses to admit that we need someone outside of ourselves to rescue and save us. We are idolaters because of our false independence. We are worshippers of ourselves because we want our truth to be king. The only way to destroy idolatry once and for all is to surrender to the King whose truth is valid and who calls us to dependency on Him and His ways.

Biblical Solutions and Application

Now that we have unraveled the layers on the component of postmodern knowledge, we can answer the opening question; why are postmoderns so skeptical about foundational objective truth? The answer is found in the developmental factors of the postmodern views on the origin, nature, and validity of knowledge. We discovered that postmodernism holds to a humanistic origin of knowledge, an experiential-based process for acquiring knowledge, and a relativistic notion of the validity of knowledge. These developments have led to a fundamental shift in Western culture towards the idolatrous worship of man, for man is at the center of all that postmodernism holds dear. So, what are the biblical solutions and application for these developments? How does the Christian who resides in Western culture avoid the trap of thinking like a postmodern idolater?

First, *God is the source of all that can be or should be known.* It rightly follows then that we as Christians should hear afresh the words of Jesus in Matthew 6:33, "But seek first His kingdom and His righteousness, and all these things will be added to you." Practically speaking, here is what this looks like in your life. The pursuit of God should not just be the sum total of your 20 minute quiet time in the morning. I am not anti-quiet time, but if you are only limiting your interaction with the source of all knowledge to a wedge of time, then are you really pursuing Him? For example, let's say for the sake of argument that you sleep 8 hours a night. That leaves 16 hours in a typical day that you are awake or 960 minutes. Are you seriously going to confine your listening to the source of all knowledge to 20/960 or 2.083% of your waking hours? I guarantee that if you are giving the postmodern culture the other 97.917% that not only is your well polluted, but the source is also. I guarantee that you source more of your knowledge in social media than you do in seeking the Lord. Seek God with your whole heart. Pray without ceasing. Seek Him while He may still be found.

Second, *start lining up your beliefs with Scripture rather than the way you feel.* Remember, at heart, you are an idolater. Your feelings will betray you. The Christians who fall the hardest are often the ones who forgot that they are still sinners, who thought with pride that they had it all together. My pastor and friend, Steve Dighton, often reminded us when I worked on staff at Lenexa Baptist of this truth. He would say both from the pulpit and privately, "Don't ever forget, we are all just one step from stupid." Your beliefs must be rooted and grounded in the truth of Scripture, not in the ways of man. Many are the days in my life where I do not feel saved; however, that does not change the fact that I am. Mark my words, if you reduce what you know to be true to your feelings on any given day, your feelings will not only lead you astray, but your feelings will become your god. You will obey them and they will take you far from the truth of God's revelation.

Third, *recognize the boundaries of your knowledge and live with humility.* I believe that as followers of Christ, we all come to our Job moment. Something hideously evil happens in our lives or to those we love and we puff out our chest and demand answers from God. We demand to know *why* we are experiencing suffering. It is at that point that God speaks into our lives through the Holy Spirit and says, like He said to Job, "Who is this that darkens counsel by words without knowledge? Now gird up your loins like a man, and I will ask you, and you instruct Me! Where were you when I laid the foundations of the earth? Tell Me if you have understanding."[5] It is at this point that we should back away slowly and simply fall on our faces. The fuel for idolatry is pride. We are really good at pride. It would do us well to recognize that there are certain things that we not only do not know, but we should not know. Humility is needed.

We began this chapter with a simple definition of postmodernism: a set of beliefs about knowledge, freedom, and language which are grounded in the rejection or modification of the modern notions of these ideas. We have asked the important question, why is postmodernism so skeptical about foundational, objective truth? Simply put, they do not believe that such a concept exists. Hopefully, we have exposed where a postmodern view of knowledge leads. It directs the human heart to the idol of human feelings and emotions, which wax and wane in the never-ending chaos of a culture in the midst of a precipitous fall. Next, we turn to the issue of freedom.

5. Job 38:2–4.

2

The Postmodern Illusion of Freedom

Postmodern Freedom: A Star Wars Trash Compactor

ONE OF MY FAVORITE movies of all time is Star Wars. No, not the prequels with the weirdness that is Jar Jar Binks, but the original 1977 version of Luke Skywalker wondering what life in the universe is all about as he stares off into the deserts of Tatooine. In one particular stressful scene, Luke and his friends are trapped in a trash compactor while trying to rescue Princess Leia. As the walls start to close in on them, Luke is pulled underneath the trash filled water by some unknown creature. He manages to escape, but the walls continue to close in until the faithful droid R2D2 finds the right switch to rescue the heroes. Quickly, the walls start to move outward while Luke and his friends begin to splash around and celebrate.

Postmodernism's views on human freedom are similar to a Star Wars trash compactor. They believe the walls of morality that restrict their freedom to act in any way that brings pleasure should

The Postmodern Illusion of Freedom

not exist. When they feel the walls of morality start to creep in on them, they cry out for someone to rescue them from restrictions on freedom. But, once the walls of morality are removed, they unknowingly celebrate in a sea of moral trash and sewage, completely unaware that at any moment they might be swallowed by an even worse monster lurking underneath the surface. Chewbacca will not be there to save them. After all, Wookies have a rock solid moral code and are pretty good judges of character.

This chapter will interact with how modern views on radical individual freedom have evolved into postmodernism's views of freedom within community. The central point here is rooted in the postmodern rejection of authority in favor of shared equality and relationship in community. My desire is for you to think about the following question; why is postmodernism enamored with the equality of outcomes for humanity? I believe that the answer is found in postmodernism's distaste for radical individual freedom birthed in the Enlightenment. In other words, the dissatisfaction with what society achieved (or did not achieve) as a result of holding up freedom as an idol has led them to sprint towards the opposite end of the spectrum, the false worship of the idealized and secularized brotherhood of man. Luke Skywalker has now been joined by a crowd staring off into the distance, wondering what we will become together.

Freedom is a Terrible God

Let me begin with a caveat. I am proud to be an American. The ballad of Lee Greenwood echoes deep in my soul. My grandfather Carl landed on the beaches of Normandy and fought in France during WWII. My great uncle Charles survived the South Pacific campaigns. My 17 year old son Chase is poised to enter boot camp and become a Marine very soon. I treasure the sacrifices many have paid in order to secure our freedom. I love being able to worship on Sunday morning without sneaking into a building with double-paned sound proof windows and lookout guards on the street. I treasure the privilege of speaking my conscience even though at times it makes reading Facebook posts unbearable. However, there are some who turn freedom into a false god.

Allow me to illustrate once again from the decade which perfected the worship of individual freedom. Case in point, the Wall Street power stock broker of the early 1980's. You can picture them now with their suspenders, red power ties, and two inch thick cell phones, drinking champagne and smoking cigars as their latest multi-million dollar deal closed. We might safely assume that tucked away in their office drawer was a picture of a sneering Gordon Gecko, offering them a hallucinated aristocratic wink of approval. Overnight, it appeared that the elites of America were chosen not on the basis of their family name or land that they owned, but by their achievements reflected through the number of zeros on their paychecks.

The freedom to achieve is an admirable right, but when wedded to radical individualism through vows of greed and success at any cost it becomes an insatiable false god. It is true that once radical individualism takes root in a culture, the decline and eventual collapse of any sense of morality is not far behind. Unbridled demand for liberty as a fundamental ethic divorced from a biblical worldview will always lead to deeper and deeper levels of cultural immorality. Robert H. Bork, writing in the mid-1990's, gave us a clear, prophetic warning we must heed.

> Our modern, virtually unqualified, enthusiasm for liberty forgets that liberty can only be "the space between the walls," the walls of morality and the law based upon morality. It is sensible to argue about how far apart the walls should be set, but it is cultural suicide to demand all space and no walls.[1]

What Bork put his finger upon is not only true philosophically, but it is also relevant pragmatically to the church. How can I make such a statement? I can sit before you as a pastor of ten years and cite case after case where the craving for liberty has led to immoral behavior in the church that has destroyed interpersonal

---

1. Bork, *Slouching Towards Gomorrah*, 65.

relationships, vocational callings, and marital bonds. Even as I sit and write these words today, blog posts are running rampant over another pastor of a large church being force to resign because of alcohol. Time and time again I have heard the argument made, "But pastor, I am free to _____. The Bible doesn't explicitly say not to _____." Feel free (no pun intended) to insert the most common phrases you hear in the blanks, "drink, smoke, watch whatever I want, etc." Again, it is fair to discuss how far apart the trash compactor walls should be, but Christian brother or sister, should you even step one foot in the trash compactor?

The problem is that in the years following the 1980's, our culture recognized that this god of achievement and individualistic freedom did not and could not ultimately satisfy our appetites. It kept demanding more and more allegiance, pushing the finishing line of success to a point which no one could possibly hope to reach. In an interesting twist, the American culture began to embrace an ethic of radical egalitarianism, shunning individual recognition and distinction for participation trophies handed out by the false god of community consciousness. After all, everyone should have the privilege of winning.

Postmoden Slavery to Community: Scientology Mission Trips

The ratio of ridiculous to relevant snail mail that I receive as a Southern Baptist professor is directly proportional to the number of times Nicholas Cage has made a terrible movie in the last ten years. In case you do not get the comparison, allow me to be explicit. I get a lot of bizarre mail. Please forgive me if you truly love Nic Cage. I still firmly believe that *National Treasure* is his best work, but that was 2004. Most of the snail mail I get ends up in the trash, although if confession is good for the soul, some of the more interesting pieces end up shoved under our Criminal Justice professor's door.

For the past two years, I have received the monthly installment of *Freedom* magazine. If you are not familiar with this publication, it is the official update for those who are members of or interested in the Church of Scientology. For the record and our trustees who may be reading this book, yes, I am a Southern Baptist professor and preacher that has affirmed the Baptist Faith and Message. No, I have never had my electrodermal activity audited by Tom Cruise.

One of the hallmarks of a successful college professor is intellectual curiosity. That is my fancy way of saying that I thumb through the Scientology magazine every month before passing it off anonymously to Brady. You guessed correctly, Brady teaches Criminal Justice at Hannibal LaGrange University and his door is near my mailbox. He also has a lot of connections to local law enforcement. Maybe I should start sliding the mail under the Biology professor's door? By the way, never let anyone convince you that college professors live a boring life. We know how to party.

One particular month as I was perusing the importance of E-meters and the benefits of psychological auditing, I turned the page to find an article on a group of young college age Scientologists who were building homes and digging wells in sub-Saharan Africa. The pictures which accompanied the piece grabbed my attention. I will be so bold as to say that if the pictures of these college students were placed on the same table as pictures from a Southern Baptist youth mission trip, you would not be able to tell the difference between the two groups.

My first response was disgust. Who does this false religion think they are, stealing tried and true Southern Baptist methods for doing missions? The revulsion quickly turned to repentance. Who do we think we are offering a false sense of community revitalization divorced from the proclamation of the gospel of Jesus Christ? Please understand, I am in complete support of improving infrastructure and providing clean drinking water to remote villages. But when such an endeavor is separated from evangelism and discipleship, we create a false god centered on the worship of our own good works baptized in a spirit of radical egalitarianism and secular humanism. Without the person of Jesus and his power to transform lives, our mission efforts would look no different than

The Postmodern Illusion of Freedom

the ones in the pages of the latest Scientology magazine. I am certain that no one is ready to ordain John Travolta as a deacon.

My illustration exists to make an important claim. Postmodernism is concerned with the restraint of individualism and the advancement of community where the goal is the equality of outcomes for all of its members. This aim is the central commandment a postmodernist must never violate. To be fair, the Bible is also concerned with the restraint of freedom and the promotion of corporeal realties, but for very different reasons. I will have more to say on this later in the chapter.

I see this truth played out consistently in the college students that I advise and mentor. They desire their lives to count. They want to make a positive contribution to society at the cost of their parent's dreams of them earning a large paycheck. Thom and Jess Rainer note these realities in their research on Millennials.

> They are the generation that seeks to bring people together. They work toward family unity. They work at jobs that make a difference in society. They are concerned about the environment, but they avoid extremism on both sides of the issue. They are a serving generation, putting other's needs before themselves.[2]

This attitude that Rainer describes is a glorious reality, if directed and attached to a biblical worldview. However, when such thinking is infected with a growing secularism and humanism as is pervasive in Western culture, the outcome is for young people to sacrifice their lives to the mantra of making humanity great again, an impossible task and a tragic false god. So, how did we get to this point? What factors have led us to this precipice of slavery to radical equality? I believe there are several causes, but three stand out as pillars in the temple of our Western god of community consciousness: the media, the educational system, and the church. I know that the last one in the list made you raise your eyebrows, but trust me, the church is not immune from the dangers of postmodern secularism.

---

2. Rainer, *The Millennials*, 167.

Radical Equality in The Goonies

June 7, 1985 was a watershed moment in Western history. It was the day *The Goonies* was released in movie theaters. I was an impressionable 14 years old. I do not believe it to be an exaggeration to say that outside of my parents and the Bible that Steven Spielberg has tremendously influenced my life. Even now, rumors are swirling of a *Goonies 2* sequel with the return of the original cast. Please say, for the love and sanctity of my childhood memories, that this is one of the Internet's greatest falsehoods.

The Goonies works so well cinematically not just because it is a great story, but because of the relationships of the characters. Each person is a misfit, incapable of achieving much on their own, but when they are forced to work together they comprise an unstoppable force. Whether it is Mouth translating Spanish on the treasure map, Andy playing the right chord on the skeleton organ, or Chunk showing up with Sloth to save the day at the end, the nonconformist are great when forced through life circumstances to conform to the code, "Goonies never say die." The group would not have advanced very far if Andy had decided to take the ride in the basket up the well instead of sending Troy's letter jacket.

Little did I know that such an incredible movie had so much to do with the birth pains of radical equality within Western society. What the movie embodied was a nascent radical egalitarianism, that is, the giving up of individual control for the sake of the greater good of the whole, where, in this case, the greater good is the preservation of their homes. This agenda is nothing less than the pursuit of the brotherhood of humanity clothed in a self-righteous community consciousness. And remember, I love *The Goonies*. Please do not get me started on *Xanadu*. Roller disco and Olympian gods are non-complementarian.

Someone at this point might say, "What is the big deal? Are you saying that we should deny the possibility of equal outcomes for members of a Western society? Are we not really *better* when we work together?" No, I am not saying that we should not work together or push for a corporate understanding of humanity. What

The Postmodern Illusion of Freedom

I am saying is that the push for greater and greater equality of outcomes evolved from equal rights has led and will continue to lead to in the Western culture a truncated view of the very definition of morality. In other words, as our culture further embraces radical egalitarianism as a major tenant of postmodernism, we will experience a demand from the masses for an increased acceptance of immorality. This reality, not possibility, is a terrifying false god which will insist on the complete submission of its worshippers on the altar of tolerance.

The false idol of radical equality opens the door to a bottomless pit of immorality with a precipitous slippery slope. Who would have imagined thirty years ago that we would see the transformation of a male sports icon into a woman? And not only see it play out before our eyes, but celebrated with the expectation that we as a society stand and clap for his courage and bravery. Our media only further advances the postmodern agenda, criticizing the evangelical Christian as one who needs to open their mind.

Just so we are clear, you can have equal rights without equal outcomes for all parties involved. That is a little something called competition. For instance, I have an equal right to stand on a basketball court with Michael Jordan. It is safe to say that the outcome is not going to be favorable for me even if I kick and scream and demand that he let me win. He is *better* than me at basketball. That's okay, I will dunk on him every time in a New Testament Greek quiz. He has no chance if we are parsing third declension nouns. I hope you see the point. Radical egalitarianism, of which our Western media is the false prophet, will inevitably result in a tolerance of immorality that the Bible clearly speaks against and says, "No." This idol must be destroyed.

Radical Equality in the American University

My theology professor in seminary used to say, "Never criticize someone until you have listened to them sympathetically."[3] While

---

3. The reference here is to Mark DeVine, PhD who taught theology at Midwestern Baptist Theological Seminary. He is now the Associate Professor

I have only worked for a Christian university for two years, my experience with higher education spans fourteen years and three academic degrees. For good or ill, I have been completely immersed in Southern Baptist institutions during my pursuit of higher education and now my work in higher education. I say all of this before I offer a critique of Western education so you will understand that I am not only a debtor to it, but also a sympathizer.

The first class I taught in higher education was New Testament Survey at Midwestern Baptist Theological Seminary in Kansas City. We met for three hours on Monday evenings. Just as a side note, when you are a PhD student you take whatever adjunct opportunities come your way. It never pays to be picky. Adjunct teaching is never glamorous, but it pays the bills and looks great on a *curriculum vitae*. I can still remember the first night of class for two clear reasons. One, because I was sweating profusely as the class was at maximum enrollment with over fifty students. Two, because of a clarifying comment one student made as I was covering the syllabus.

If you are a college student reading this right now, may I encourage you that it is never a good idea to make a snide comment about the syllabus requirements on the first day of class. At least send a snarky email, believe me, college professors love reading them. In my case, the first night of class began rather well, that is, until I brought up the required ten page research paper due at the end of the semester. About halfway back from the front, a student slowly raised his hand. A brief sense of exhilaration arose within me. Here was my first genuine seminary student question. The enjoyment of the moment vanished as I heard these words come out of his mouth, "Don't you think that is a little too harsh to assign a ten page paper?"

---

of History and Doctrine at Beeson Divinity where I am confident he is still separating people for their preference for either puffy or crunchy Cheetos. The quote here was usually in the context of when someone in class would want bring up the Calvinist—Arminian debate. DeVine's response was usually to ask them if they had read Calvin. If they responded negatively, he would drop the quote upon them and then move on with the lecture. Or, he would say something about tying half his brain behind his back so it would be a fair fight.

The Postmodern Illusion of Freedom

I was much less sarcastic in the past than I am currently. Looking back, I should have said, "Actually, it is a little harsh, but on me since I have to read all the papers." The strength of a sarcastic comment is directly proportional to the length of time you are removed from the situation where it would be most effective. As he made the comment, a silence fell across the room and several students dropped their heads, refusing to make eye contact with me. I waited for a few seconds and responded, "No, not really, welcome to seminary."

The modern college student's descent into a sense of entitlement and radical equality of outcomes is growing worse by the year. According to Litfin, "To the postmodernist, no absolute principles, laws, values, or truths are normative or binding for all times, places, and people."[4] What Litfin is saying is that postmodernity is awash in relativism and the denial of exclusivity. In reality, postmodernism is thriving because of a latent preference for casual subjectivism, the belief that objective truth claims are to be held loosely. A worldview such as this one will always clash with the objective measurements required for a student to graduate. Radical equality of outcomes is the icing on the cake of modernity's entitlement pedigree.

We, even in the environment of a Christian university, often encounter students who expect to pass their classes simply because they are enrolled in them and have paid their tuition. Each semester, I encounter students who are surprised when they receive a failing grade for a course. Again, a helpful word of caution. If you rarely attend class, turn in half of your assignments, and skip the final exam, you are probably not going to pass my class. Call me old fashioned, I believe that you get what you earn. Faith alone will not earn you an A, you have to show me your faith by your works.

Postmodernism's thirst for a monistic view on radical inclusiveness over and against a marketplace of ideas and dialogue does not appear capable of being quenched in the current university environment. The pluralistic environment on college campuses is quickly fading in favor of a belligerent monism that demands

---

4. Litfin, *Conceiving the Christian College*, 268.

allegiance to the false god of radical egalitarianism. The worship of radical equality has found its sanctuary, the secular American university. Our young people are making their pilgrimage in ignorance, having received their psychological reconditioning in the domain of the postmodern culture.

I would argue that if students are not allowed to fail and subsequently learn from their mistakes, the outcome will not be a radical increase of equality, but a radical decline of intellect within Western society. When universities abandon the ideals of rationality and objective inquiry, society will inevitably arrive at a level of incompetency that will demand an increase of outside egalitarian control. Listen again to Bork,

> Universities now threaten to abandon those ideals [rationality and skepticism] and to instruct society to abandon them as well. As the universities lose their respect for intellect, that attitude spreads not only to lower schools but to the society at large."[5]

At this juncture, allow me to open a window of hope. I do see at the Christian university where I serve a desire for ideas and dialogue to flourish. Our campus is situated in the small community of Hannibal, Missouri. The town at large is not ethnically diverse, however, as a university we are consistently growing in our international student presence.[6] As you can imagine, not every international student who comes to us is a Christian. This reality provides opportunities for interesting discussions and the free exchange of ideas. Not to mention interesting stares from people at Wal Mart when family members of these students show up in their traditional dress.

Some at this juncture might protest and say, "Are you not, at a Christian university, demanding that your students pledge their allegiance to Jesus?" The simple answer is "No." A wide chasm

---

5. Bork, 250.

6. Currently, the percentage of international students on the campus of Hannibal LaGrange is approximately 19% of our total student population. We boast students from Europe, Africa, Southeast Asia, South America, and the Middle East.

The Postmodern Illusion of Freedom

exists between demanding that a student *must* be a Christian and persuading in the free marketplace of ideas within a university that a student *should* be a Christian. Herein lies the beauty and potential of a rejection of postmodern idolatry in the American university. While it is not entirely clear whether the university simply reflects or profoundly influences culture, one truth remains; the current university model in the West, and especially the Christian one, must refuse to lower the bar of competence simply because a postmodern god throws a fit and says we must make educational outcomes equal for all who apply.

Radical Equality in the American Church

The third pillar in Western postmodern slavery to radical equality is not one that you would expect. It is the postmodern, secularized "Christian" church. You will obviously note that I placed the word Christian in quotes. The church, as I plan to describe it in the pages that follow, may call itself "Christian," however, a vast difference exists between the terms Christian and biblical. What evidence exists for radical egalitarianism within the American church? And, if it does exist, how did we get there? It may be easiest to answer the last question first and then provide some examples of postmodern tendencies in the church. I believe the answers for understanding this shift may be seen in our discipleship.

We have experienced in the American church a shift to either one of two dangerous poles in discipleship. The first shift is the acquisition of more knowledge that results in an amputated application of the knowledge to our daily lives. For instance, it adds nothing to the kingdom of Jesus to have all the blanks and contemplated journaling filled out in your *Share Jesus without Fear* workbook if you never share the gospel with anyone. We have settled for a brand of Christianity in the West that makes us more knowledgeable regarding our own morality, but less likely to actually apply that morality to our daily behavior. The second shift is at the opposite end of the spectrum, a growing complacency with respect to biblical literacy.

The first church that I served had a tradition that after the service, the pastor would stand in the back of the sanctuary to greet people as they departed. For the most part, the comments I received were warm, encouraging to my heart as a young minister. But, on rare occasions, a comment was levied that would make anyone raise an eyebrow in confusion. I recall one particular Sunday where I stood greeting people after preaching a series on 1 and 2 Peter. A church member paused, smiled, shook my hand and said, "Great sermon pastor, but. . ." That one little word has the ability to immediately cause a pastor's stomach to do somersaults. My body stiffened for the hand grenade of criticism he was about to launch at me.

The full text of his comment was, "Great sermon pastor, but when are you going to preach on the words of Jesus?" I must have paused long enough or had a look of confusion on my face because he felt it then necessary to clarify his question. He quipped, "You know? The words of Jesus in the Bible. The words in red." Bless his heart. By the way, anytime you hear the phrase "Bless his heart," you know that nothing good is about to follow. The response that I intended to say was, "Well, technically they are all his words." But, I bit my tongue and reminded him that we were beginning a series on the Gospel of Mark soon. Biblical illiteracy is dangerous and it is growing more prevalent in our churches.

I use these two shifts in discipleship to illustrate my point about the infection of postmodernism within the Western church. Postmodernism's expectation for the rejection of objective truth fits the paradigm of discipleship that essentially says in its praxiology, "I can know a lot about a subject, but I dare not apply it lest it make me stand out among the crowd." On the other hand, postmodernism's production of a less competent society has resulted in a complacency for intellectual pursuit in the church. The rejection of objective truth and a less competent populace has produced in the church individuals who either sever their knowledge from their behavior or they shun knowledge for their behavior. Unfortunately, both of these postmodern tendencies in discipleship end up in the same place, immorality.

The Postmodern Illusion of Freedom

When did we cease, as a church, to not only *think* deeply about our faith, but also to *practice* deeply our faith? The answer might be found in the push towards a personal relationship with Jesus preached and taught in the Western church over the last sixty years. It is true to say that Jesus does have a personal relationship with each one of his children, but it is a stretch to say that when Jesus was on the cross, he was thinking about me above anyone else. The horror of the cross must never be reduced to an individualistic event. He gave his life as a ransom for many. The reductionist nature of such thinking fits well with a Western conscience, but it does not accurately reflect the biblical narrative or the theology which arises from it.

Conformity to the language of intimate personal language in soteriology is still pervasive in the church. For over half a century we have consistently heard that if we say a personal prayer or if we personally walk an aisle that our salvation is secure. What if the practice of requiring an individual to pray a personal prayer was simply born out of a superstitious church culture that was driven by the counting of decisions? Could the possibility exist that a person may walk an aisle because they are making a decision for counseling of their life situation rather than a decision to follow Jesus? I am not saying these are the summary indictments of what all of our churches are practicing. What I am saying is that these instances do exist and we must be careful in the way we speak about a person being in Christ.

I do believe that the reason we are seeing people leave the American church is because they are fed up with a superficial, personal Christianity that ironically has produced in the last thirty years very little personal and cultural change. Please hear me, this is my opinion and I bring no statistics to back up this claim. Since the American church has more often reflected the culture, we have seen it shift with the –isms that culture embodies.

For example, modernism with its Enlightenment roots in the freedom and progress of individuality mirrored the personal discipleship, seeker sensitive, and church growth movements of the 1980's and 1990's. Postmodernism is currently festering in

American churches as seen in secular progressive agendas. John Wesley may have sold his horse and went back to England if he could have foreseen the Methodist denomination's recent election of its first homosexual pastor.

Much more treatment should be given to the existence of postmodernism in the church, but for now, these examples serve our purposes well. I will certainly return to this subject later in the book. For now, we must turn once again to some biblical solutions and application to the issue of postmodernism's views on human freedom. Our penchant for the idolatry of freedom is not modern, it is ancient. We are false worshippers of an idolatrous freedom we were never intended to possess. It is time for us to smash the false idol of freedom in favor of a true biblical understanding of freedom.

Biblical Solutions and Application

At the beginning of the chapter, I asked you to think about this question, why is postmodernism so enamored with the equality of outcomes for humanity? I believe we answered this question by understanding the exchange of freedom as a false god for a radically egalitarian one. The satisfaction that the false god of freedom failed to produce in its worshippers is now being sought through slavery to an egalitarian god that cries out for tolerance and no distinctions in the whole of society. So, what does the Bible have to say about these idols that compete for the hearts of mankind?

First, the Bible reminds us that, *freedom is not the goal of your Christian life*. Let me say this truth in a different way. The aim of the Christian life is submission to the glorious service of a benevolent King. Yes, you are saved and freed from your sins. No, you are not free to live in any manner you choose, especially if it is in direct conflict with God's revealed word. The clearest teaching regarding this principle comes from the pen of the Apostle Peter. First Peter 2:16 says, "Act as free men, and do not use your freedom as a covering for evil, but use it as *slaves* of God."

The Postmodern Illusion of Freedom

Paul reminds his readers of essentially the same principle, saying in Romans 6:16, "Do you not know that when you present yourselves to someone as slaves for obedience, you are slaves of the one whom you obey?" Later, in 1 Corinthians 6:19b-20 he boldly declares, "you are not your own, for you have been bought with a price: therefore glorify God in your slave body." The evidence is clear that the biblical writers did not have in mind the principles of modern, Westernized freedom when they authored these letters to fledgling churches.

The picture Western culture paints of freedom is an idealized representation of a self-reliant individual, able to choose willingly the multiplicity of paths that are available. One can imagine a strong, barrel chested man raised to his full height, hands on his hips with one foot standing on a rock. The biblical view of freedom is antithetical to this imagined ideal. In reality, a biblical portrait of freedom would simply be a person with one knee bent in submission to a King who is ready to commission him for service. The warning bears repeating one final time; the Western idealized view of freedom is a terrible false god.

Second, *radical equality belongs in the context of the church, not the culture.* Let's listen again to Paul from Romans 12:4, "For just as we have many members in one body and all the members do not have the same function, so we who are many are one body in Christ, and individually members one of another." A little later, Paul summarizes his argument to the Roman believers in 15:6, "so that with one accord you may with one voice glorify the God and Father of our Lord Jesus Christ."

Radical egalitarianism with the goal of subjective immoral tolerance on the part of the society's members is false worship. Egalitarianism in the context of the corporate body of Christ with the goal of the glory of God among the nations is a worship the Bible encourages of us. Postmodernists did not invent radical egalitarianism, they have simply perverted its purposes in order to justify their sinful desires. The Bible does promote the equality of humanity, but not underneath the banner of secular tolerance. It asks humanity to surrender their individual rights for participation in, as 1 Peter 2:9 describes, "A chosen race, a royal priesthood, a people for God's own possession."

These twin deities of freedom and radical equality have not only dominated Western culture, they have also infected the church. It is time, as painful as it might be, to purge the infection and for God's people to not just start living differently, but biblically. Until Christians in the postmodern culture begin shunning their rights and embracing their corporate identity as God's inheritance, we will continue to watch the culture slip deeper into horrific levels of immorality. I am not saying that it will be easy to smash these idols. I am saying that it is necessary.

3

The Postmodern Game of Language

The Importance of Language

ONE OF THE MOST difficult aspects of studying linguistics is that you have to use the very thing you are talking about (language) to describe what you are talking about (language). This principle was embedded in my conscience and life for a little more than five years as I researched and wrote my dissertation on linguistic metaphor in 2 Corinthians. Okay, take a deep breath. This chapter is not going to require you to wrap your mind around the signalling and syntactical configuration of active metaphors. On the other hand, if that is what you have been waiting for your whole life, I will gladly email you a copy of my dissertation.[1]

Language is funny, especially in the realm of metaphor. For example, consider the power that the little word "like" has in our English language. If I were to express the sentence, "Sam is *like*

---

1. Turner, *The Signalling and Syntactical Configuration of Active Metaphors: 2 Corinthians 10:1–6 as a Test Case*. The content of this chapter draws heavily upon my dissertation research, including many of the examples of how language works.

a woman," you would understand that Sam shares some characteristics of women in general. Perhaps he might cry at romantic movies or carry around a murse.[2] Now, if I were to leave out the word "like" in the sentence and say, "Sam *is* a woman," you might be tempted towards a very different interpretation. Sam could be shorthand for Samantha, literally meaning that Sam is a woman with a unisex name. Or, given our current cultural climate, Sam could be a man who is now a woman. Language is funny.

Even though we may quibble over the interpretations associated with linguistic constructions, one crucial area we must avoid is the tendency within postmodernism to speak of religious discourse as subjective. Another way of saying this is to state the opposite of the postmodern subjective principle, namely, objective religious discourse is neither modern or postmodern, it is biblical. This chapter will dialogue with the question; why is postmodernism fascinated with how we speak about god?

These language games are critical to understand with respect to the veiled nature of idolatry in our Western culture. In other words, the more enamored we become with subjective dialogue about god, the likelihood that we are creating a god of our own and not the One we find in the pages of Scripture is greater. The sections ahead will reveal that the religious-language game brought to life within postmodernism is nothing more than a culturally nuanced excuse for worshipping a plurality of gods.

The Prayers of "Old Tom"

The first church I pastored had two men named Tom, one young and one old. The young one was simply known as Tom while the older took the title, old Tom. The designation was not meant in an offensive manner, it was just how they were distinguished. Old Tom was about 70 when I came to the church. I soon learned in a unique way that he was a new Christian. Like most Southern

---

2. For those who do not know the definition of a murse, it is a small manpurse usually worn by hipsters at a local urban coffee shop. In some contexts, a murse can refer to a male nurse. See, I told you that language was funny.

The Postmodern Game of Language

Baptist churches, there is a point in every service where the offering is collected. The typical pattern is for one of the men who are taking up the offering to pray. I will never forget the first time I heard old Tom pray.

Old Tom prayed from his heart. The trained Baptist mantras were noticeably absent from his prayers. If you have attended a Baptist church for any length of time, you know exactly what I mean. Old Tom did not know the phrase "Bless the gift and the giver." He never felt the need for switching to King James English. It was beautiful because his prayers were from his heart and not his heritage.

The games we play at church with prayer are hazardous, particularly when it comes to language. We are taught to recite words or phrases, but we do not often think about their meaning or significance with respect to theology. If we are not careful, a sanitized religious subjectivism will creep into our disciplines. This pitfall is especially acute with the practice of prayer. The memorized mantras produce a wonderful subjective experience, scratching the liturgical itch of a rich tradition. However, it is linguistic suicide to divorce the language of prayer, or any religious language for that matter, from its objective foundations. To do so may result in the worship of the prayer itself or even the one who is praying.

Here is another way to think about the importance of religious language. I can read Spanish, but I do not understand what I am reading. The simple reason is that I only took four years of Spanish, twenty seven years ago. I have the ability to pick up a book written in Spanish and I can read it with all of the inflected nuances of Antonio Banderas. It produces a rich, subjective feeling of once again being in Señor DeLuca's class sitting next to Steve Dixon talking about everything but Spanish. You understand that I can have the experience of reading Spanish apart from an understanding of Spanish. The same is true of religion.

You can attend a church service and have an incredible experience. The music can move you, the prayers warm your heart, and the sermon engage your mind. You can walk away with a great appreciation of all things religious, but still lack an objective understanding of what was being sung, prayed, or preached. Truthfully, you are no better off than if you just walked out of a Justin Bieber concert. Modernism's attempt to kill the objective nature of religious language failed. Postmodernism, on the other hand, does not want to keep religious language in the grave. Their desire is to resurrect religious language, albeit with a much different goal. The aim within postmodernism is to talk at length about religion.

Postmodern Religious Speech

Postmodernism has perfected how we speak, or rather, how little we speak about God. Remember that two of the pillars of postmodern thinking are a willingness to sacrifice reason for being open to new ideas and of course, a militant tolerance for accepting another person's worldview. At the heart of this new way of speaking about religion is an inconsistent, truncated view of what may be potentially defined by another person as morally right or wrong. Postmodern thinkers demand acceptance of their ideas absent of objective judgments over whether their claims are true or false.

The result of such a worldview is inconsistent responses by postmoderns in the realm of ethics. It is not terribly difficult to prove this claim against postmodernism. Anyone who has spent a significant amount of time on social media understands perfectly the inconsistencies in personal ethics. I dare you to try and make an objective truth claim against someone's postmodern Facebook post. You will quickly discover a mob that will disparage your lack of tolerance and question your arrogance over showing your friend the error of his ways. For this reason, I will always abstain from truth claim debates on Facebook.

Truth claims are objective. More importantly, truth objectively exists apart from cultural influence. Consider the wonder of flying for 14 hours in an airplane from Shanghai to Chicago. If you were to ask most people what route the flight would likely take, they would draw a straight line from the Chinese coast through the Western coast of the United States. However, the best route

The Postmodern Game of Language

for such a flight is to hug the coast of Russia and fly over the Bering Straits through Alaska and Canada. The reason this route is the best is because of the curvature of the Earth. The shape of the Earth is an objective truth that is experienced by all regardless of culture. No pilot is going to take the straight route from Shanghai to Chicago. The plane will run out of fuel.

I believe that the Earth is round because it is objectively true. A postmodern thinker would never say, "The Earth is not round because I do not believe it to be round." However, this contradiction is exactly what they are saying when they deny the reality of an opponent's belief in objective truth. Postmodernists rage against foundational objective truth claims. They prefer, rather, to speak about pluralistic realities in which competing truth claims may live in harmony and without the fear of objective challenges. What matters most for a postmodern thinker is the preservation of an individual's understanding and validity of their beliefs. These tenets of postmodernism have far reaching implications in theology.

First, postmodern religious speech denies the exclusive truth claims of God as revealed in the Bible. We read in Jeremiah 10:10 that, "the Lord is the true God; He is the living God and the everlasting King." Later, in the same context, we are told, "Every man is stupid, devoid of knowledge; every goldsmith is put to shame by his idols; for his molten images are deceitful, and there is no breath in them." These verses make strong objective truth claims. According to a postmodernist, if I believe these statements made by Jeremiah, then they become part of my beliefs. Therefore, they must be accepted and tolerated by others within the pluralistic, religious marketplace. May I just say that this logic does not line up with reality?

Do you remember the game of charades in the Buddhist temple? Imagine how different the situation might have been had I pointed my finger at the Buddhist monk and told him, "You are stupid. You are devoid of knowledge. You are put to shame by your golden statue. There is no breath in it." How do you think he might react? You certainly would not expect him to have a typical postmodern response. He would never say, "Your truth is legitimate.

After all, you really believe it to be true, so it must be true. I will show tolerance towards your pluralistic contribution to the marketplace of religious ideas." No, in reality, he would probably find his friends and seek to do me bodily harm. Are you beginning to see the ridiculous results of carrying postmodern thinking to its logical conclusion?

Second, postmodern religious speech loves to dialogue about god, but refuses to acknowledge the unique truth claims of Jesus. It is perfectly acceptable in a postmodern setting to discuss religion or even god, but the moment someone brings up Jesus, the personal distaste for the conversation changes faster than the latest hashtag trend on Twitter. Postmodernists are fascinated with the way we speak about god, because speaking only about god is safe and supportive of a pluralistic worldview. To reduce the identity of god through subjective nomenclature means that I can dialogue with a Muslim or a Buddhist about religion in safety and security. Again, this false idol of subjective religious speech does not match the realities that are faced by us in the culture.

I am certainly welcome to have an open conversation with a local imam about religion or even religious issues related to social justice. In our Western culture, we might find common ground on combatting modern day slavery or even the identity of an unborn fetus as a person. Nevertheless, even with common religious pluralistic overlap, I do not believe for one second that the local imam would allow me to preach John 14:6 from his pulpit. Nor would he expect me to allow him to preach Yusif Ali 3:59 before my local Baptist congregation.[3] You can see that although we possess similar religious speech, we hold different, objective truth claims on the person of Jesus Christ.

The end game for postmodernism is an eternal moratorium on the discussion or establishment of objective truth claims. This postmodern desire for pluralistic religious speech is a slippery

---

3. This passage from the Qur'an teaches that Jesus was created by God in the same way that Adam was, out of dust. It reads, "The similitude of Jesus before Allah is that of Adam; He created him from dust, then said to him: 'Be.' And he was."

The Postmodern Game of Language

idol that if not put in check will eventually infect the church. The results will be an increased demand for tolerance not only in the culture, but in the household of the Living God. My prediction is that if this postmodern idolatry continues, we may see acceptance of immoral behavior in the church that would make the Corinthians throw up in the back of their mouths. The time has come for Christ followers to stand for objective truth. The obvious question we must ask next is, how does a person persuade a postmodernist that they are wrong?

Michael Scott: The Postmodern Jesus

I hope you would agree that if the idols inherent in postmodern religious speech are to be destroyed, then it is going to require clear communication of the gospel. In Season 6, Episode 12 of *The Office*, Michael Scott dresses up as Jesus at the annual Christmas party. As a side note, if you have never seen *The Office*, you might want to update the queue on your Netflix profile and start watching.

Michael's motivation to play Jesus is out of anger that Phyllis was chosen by Jim to be the Secret Santa instead of him. Toby protests against Michael and is called the anti-Christ. Stanley is called out publicly for his adultery. At the end of it all on a conference call with his boss, Michael describes Jesus as having the power of flight and the ability to heal leopards. By the way, his version of Jesus preaches forgiveness, but not forgetfulness, especially in the case of Jim breaking the Secret Santa tradition.

The point here is that this portrayal, while good for comedic ratings, is also indicative of the confusion in our culture surrounding the person of Jesus. May I burst an evangelistic bubble for you? A massive chasm exists between our historically objective, Baptist evangelistic methodology and postmodern culture. Please do not misunderstand me at this point. I am not arguing for an abolishment of the Romans Road. What I am saying is that we as Christian thinkers must be willing to begin at a different place with postmodernists. In order to abolish postmodern religious speech, we must cross the divide and exercise great patience as light slowly breaks through the pluralistic, cultural darkness. I truly believe that clearly communicating the gospel to a Western postmodernist is akin to sharing with an Eastern Chinese atheist.

According to my friends who have worked on the mission field in Southeast Asia for nine years, on average it takes a Chinese person two years to solidify their faith in Jesus Christ. The main reason is because the starting point is different for a Chinese person than the one historically practiced in the West. One cannot begin with the cross of Jesus when sharing the gospel with an average Chinese atheist. You have to begin with the existence of God. Once this fact is established, the existence of God must be aligned with the God of the Bible. This method takes time and probably more perseverance than we are willing to give.

I would submit to you that the starting point in communicating the gospel with a postmodernist is no different than that of an average Chinese person. Postmodernism is functionally atheistic and as a result, humanistic in its praxiology. This reality may cause you to consider evangelizing postmoderns as an impossible endeavor. May I encourage you that it is not a hopeless cause, it is just awkward. We stumble because postmodernists often ask questions that are not found in our pocket gospel tracts.

The reason postmodern evangelism feels weird is because it is not the way we were taught in the church to communicate the gospel. Furthermore, we are not instructed in the biblical principle of evangelistic sowing and reaping as in 1 Corinthians 3: 6–7. Paul tells us, "I planted, Apollos watered, but God was causing the growth." This truth should produce humility in us as we seek to communicate the gospel, particularly when gospel proclamation is directed towards postmodern skepticism. Allow me to further illustrate this principle by taking you to the side of a Tibetan mountain.

Danger! Do Not Touch the Yak!

Have you ever come into contact with a live yak? I have. They are interesting creatures and in case you are wondering, they are also

The Postmodern Game of Language

delicious. My first international mission trip to the Tibetan regions of Shangri-La included the responsibility of watching over two young ladies from Lenexa Baptist, the infamous sister combination known as Morgan and Taylor. As interns for our mission pastor, they earned the privilege of going on the trip. In the months leading up to our departure, their mother consistently reminded me to keep them safe and out of trouble. If you know these two young ladies, well, you know.

One of Morgan's dreams was to have her picture taken with a live yak. Folks, this is ministry, you cannot make this stuff up. A portion of our trip was centered on seeing the sights in Shangri-La as tourists, which included a cable car ride up the Shika Snow Mountains to a summit of 15,000 feet. Thankfully, the cable car stops halfway up the mountains so you can literally catch your breath before continuing to the top. It was at this point in the journey that Morgan and Taylor noticed a herd of yaks grazing on the side of the mountain. They handed me their cameras and proceeded to walk towards a solitary yak approximately 100 yards away.

As I was figuring out the proper camera angle for the best shot possible, I heard from behind me a Chinese man shouting in English, "No! Dangerous! Dangerous!" I turned to see a middle-aged Chinese man running towards me with his arms in the air. Once he reached me he pointed at Morgan and Taylor and said, "Don't touch. Yaks are very dangerous." You can imagine my surprise at this new revelation, but also the fact that a Chinese man was speaking English to me in the Tibetan wilderness. For the record, I conveniently left out this story for Morgan and Taylor's parents. Sorry Irene, they were just too stubborn.

Once my shock had worn off, I began to engage this new friend in conversation. I asked his name. He proudly gave me his English name, Frank.[4] My heart jumped in my chest as I recognized an opportunity to share the gospel with Frank. To the best of my recollection, here is how the conversation went.

---

4. Chinese nationals who are learning English will often take an American name. As you can see, this sets up some interesting encounters.

"Frank, it is great to meet you. Where are you from?" I said, smiling.

"Oh," he quickly replied, "I am from Beijing."

"Your English is very good. Where did you learn to speak English?"

Frank answered, "I learned at the university. I am a professor here with my students."

I nodded in approval because I knew that I now had a bridge to the gospel with this new friend, our yak protector. Expediently, I began to cross the bridge to the gospel. "Frank," I said, "I am also a teacher."

Frank's eyes widened in surprise. "What do you teach?"

I took a deep breath. It was about to get real. "I teach the Bible. Have you ever read the Bible?"

Lowering his head, Frank responded, "Yes, but it is very hard to understand."

Looking around us at the beauty of God's creation, I pressed Frank, "Isn't this place beautiful? How do you think all of this came to be?"

Frank shook his head and said, "I don't know. I guess God made it."

At this point my mind and heart were leaping. He understands the principle of natural revelation! Romans 1:20 is right! Just as I was prepared to launch into the argument for the gospel from creation, Frank's students arrived. Distracted, he thanked me for talking with him. I thanked him for saving us from a yak massacre. We separated and the conversation ended.

Here is what I want to impress upon you. Some might read the transcript of my conversation with Frank and write it off as an unsuccessful evangelistic attempt. Nothing could be further from the truth. Two points deserve to be highlighted. First, I was able to begin the conversation at the point where Frank was at spiritually. In Christian speak, Frank was not ready for meat, he was still trying to digest milk. Second, God allowed me to plant a seed in Frank's heart. My prayer for Frank, and others that I have encountered, is that someone else would come along and water the seed of the gospel. And, ultimately, that God would cause the growth.

May I be so bold at this juncture to say that if God can use a yak as a gospel conversation starter, then he can use you to communicate the gospel to a postmodern, pluralistic, humanistic idolater? You must get past the awkwardness of such a task. You must realize that the conversations are going to be messy. You need to accept that the cookie cutter Baptist Sunday School answers just will not satisfy the postmodern inquisitive, skeptical mind. Be encouraged. Start a conversation. Find out where the person is at spiritually and meet them there. Plant gospel seeds; sow them abundantly. Pray for others to water. Be patient and persevere. Trust God to provide the growth.

Subjective Contradictions: The Walking Dead

I have a confession to make. I have seen every episode of AMC's *The Walking Dead*. For those who live under a cultural rock, the series is perhaps the most watched show on television the last six years. Yes, it is gory and disgusting. Death from zombies or other humans is a constant reality. I watch the show with my teenage boys. I consider it more of a training video than entertainment. Honestly, I watch it with them because it provides opportunities for conversations about morality. Plus, everyone on some level loves seeing zombies get killed in creative ways each week.

The Walking Dead is not about zombies, it is about humans. The zombies are just fodder and filler for the real struggle that is occurring among the characters. The show's underlying premise, in my humble opinion, is a treatise on what humanity would do to one another if all of society's laws and morality were suddenly removed. In other words, it is a show that has at its core the total depravity of humanity. I am not giving anything away when I say that more often than not, Rick Grimes and his friends have more to fear from other people than they do from the walkers (zombies).

The scenarios that are set up in the show raise the question of where the line of morality should or should not end. The main character, Rick, is consistently portrayed as one who struggles with the decision to take or spare a person's life. For those who have seen the show, you know exactly what I am referencing. Rick, for instance, has no problem biting the jugular of a man in lieu of potential heinousness about to be levied at his son Carl; however, he struggles with the decision to kill the character known simply as the Governor. Again, for the sake of reference for those lacking knowledge, the Governor is a character that makes Charles Manson look like Winne the Pooh.

The series does an incredible job of revealing the tension within these characters over their struggle to find a consistent morality. I am sure this dilemma is one that is intended by the writers. It paints a clear picture of the risks associated with postmodern subjectivism. As Christians who believe that objective truth exists, we must be prepared to point out these subjective contradictions for our postmodern friends. This practice will unmask their warped worldview and generate pressure which can only be relieved through the reconciliation of their postmodern inconsistencies with the objective truth of the gospel. Returning to *The Walking Dead*, our voice should be that of Morgan Jones (peace and reason) and not Rick Grimes (chaos and insanity).

Biblical Solutions and Application

The question that we sought to answer in this chapter was, why is postmodernism fascinated with how we speak about god? The answers uncovered were complicated and variegated with respect to the postmodern game of language. Furthermore, we have now seen the connections between postmodern language games and idolatry. When pluralism and subjective truth rise up within a culture, the outcome is always the tolerance of numerous false gods.

This chapter established the postmodernist's need and desire to bury once and for all objective religious language. This foundational element within postmodernism revealed further a longing to deny the validity of any absolute truth claims, especially the ones found in the pages of Scripture. Finally, I addressed the reluctance

The Postmodern Game of Language

of Christians to engage postmoderns with a clear presentation of the gospel even when clear subjective contradictions exist in their worldview. Now, it is important to consider some biblical solutions and application to this postmodern language circus.

First, *theology is not just for the seminarian, it is for every Christ follower.* Phillips, echoing the thoughts of Wittgenstein, said, "Theology is the grammar of religious discourse."[5] As a linguist, I disagree with much found in these authors, but Phillips quote bears truth we should hear. The point I believe they are making is that how we speak to one another about our religious beliefs reveals our theology. In that case, whether you want to admit it or not, you are a theologian.

Unfortunately, the average church pew sitter gives very little thought to theology. They put forth an argument that goes something like this, "Theology is for people that go to seminary. Our pastor went to seminary. We pay him to be the theologian." That's all well and good if your pastor's theology is rooted in the objective truth of Scripture. The reality is that you might have a functional heretic leading your congregation. A word of caution is necessary after what I just said. There is a big difference between your pastor preaching heresy and preaching against the sin in your life. Please extinguish the torch and put down the pitchfork.

What will it take for the average Christian to love theology? I submit that it will involve the lost art of reading. If my daughter could read and understand *Mere Christianity* at ten years old, what is your excuse? The commitment might be for you to put down the cell phone and pick up the Bible and read. I challenge you that if you are truly serious about avoiding the slide into cultural, postmodern idolatry, then you will start doing life differently. Expand not merely your breadth of reading choices, but also your depth. Read authors that challenge you to think deeply about the things of God. Ask your pastor. He will thank you after he recovers from his fainting spell.

Second, *build your life on the truth claims of the Bible.* The person who is most immune from the disease of idolatry is the one

---

5. Phillips, *Wittgenstein and Religion*, 4.

who is inoculated with the objective truth of God's infallible, inerrant Word. By the way, the quickest way to an "Amen" in preaching is to drop those two adjectives in a sermon. I want to impress on you the crucial importance of taking the correct posture with respect to the Bible. In other words, we must not stand over the Bible, picking the parts that we like over the ones we dislike. The truth is, there are many verses in the Bible that I find difficult to swallow. Rather, we should stand under the authority of the Bible. Where its truth claims conflict with our feelings, we adjust our lives accordingly.

One of my friends in ministry, Kent Hackathorn, used to have an interesting job. Before his role as Associate Pastor at Lenexa Baptist, Kent worked at the Federal Reserve Bank in Kansas City. He would describe to us how they would push around carts filled with money day after day. I believe that Kent has probably looked at more money than most people will in their entire life. As a result, he is able to spot forged currency quicker than the lip syncing of Milli Vanilli. You see, he spent so much time looking at what was real, that spotting a counterfeit became easy.

I am going to encourage you that this Hackathorn principle needs to be yours with respect to the objective truth claims of Scripture. Idolatry always warps the truth of God. Therefore, if your goal is to avoid the postmodern pit of idolatry, then you must spend the majority of your time in what is true, the Bible, so that when the culture presents you with a false alternative you will be able to spot it immediately. Idolatry is subtle and sneaky, but I guarantee that the hidden word of God in your heart wielded by the indwelt Holy Spirit will always cause you to pause over the temptations presented by a postmodern culture.

Finally, *Christ followers must be open to new evangelistic strategies.* Our Western culture is confused about Jesus, but they are not without hope of being reached with the gospel. It is time for Christ followers to reevaluate their relationships and conversations with postmodern neighbors, family members, co-workers, and friends. New lines of communication must be opened. Can I urge you not to open the dialogue with, "So, you are a postmodernist? Hope

The Postmodern Game of Language

you know that you are an idolater." Cultural offensiveness is a poor and unbiblical strategy. The gospel will do a good job of offending people without your ignorance.

Your aim should center on having conversations with people. No, I am not talking about responding to a Facebook post. Gospel communication with a postmodernist is best done face-to-face. Go to a coffee shop, but please shun the local tavern. Postmodernists are already confused in their thinking, adding alcohol will not help. It is important that you are prepared for anything, surprised by nothing, and in no way offended by everything a postmodern might offer. Ask good questions. For example, "Why do you believe what you believe?" is a great response for those encapsulated in postmodern ideology. You must be prepared to meet the person where they are spiritually and philosophically. To do so is to reveal a commitment in your heart to sow seeds of the gospel in the postmodern soil. You never know when or how the gospel will expose the hidden idolatry in the lives of those you love like Jesus.

4

The Biblical Diagnosis of the Human Heart

The Wisdom of Elrond

IT IS ARGUABLE THAT the hopeless portrait painted in previous chapters about idolatry in our postmodern culture is a new challenge that we face. However, as we transition from the reasons idolatry exists in a postmodern culture to the biblical ones, we will discover that the problem is much older. Idolatry is not a new trend, externally manifested by a culture. It is an inward sickness, internally hidden in the heart of every person. Idolatry, if not destroyed, will consume us and direct our lives, fulfilling its evil purposes while convincing us that it is small, harmless, and common.

I have lost track of how many times I have read Tolkien's *The Lord of the Rings*. Great works of literature are not meant to just be read, but to be read again and again, digesting the truths that they offer to our hearts and minds. Even now, as I type these words, I am listening to the soundtracks from the movie on my Spotify playlist. If you argue that all you need to do is see the movie, then you are lacking in wisdom. The books have so many more characters and

The Biblical Diagnosis of the Human Heart

nuances that the movies could never possibly contain. I am still upset at Peter Jackson that he left out Tom Bombadil.

The crux of Tolkien's narrative, of course, centers on the destruction of the Ring of Power. We see throughout the books how a small, common gold ring affects those with whom it comes into contact. Bilbo, Frodo, Gandalf, Galadriel, Gollum, and Boromir all come under the spell of the malevolent trinket sought by the evil Sauron. Each one is tempted to take the ring and treasure it for themselves. Some pass the test and others fail. The ring changes people, often placing them in a lurid trance from which they struggle to escape.

The ring becomes a symbol for trusting in something that looks good, but we observe as the story unfolds that even in moral people it eventually produces great evil. The wisdom of Elrond, the elf king of Rivendell and one of the oldest characters in the story, concerning the ring is given early in the first book. He remarks that Isildur should not have taken the ring after it was cut from Sauron's hand, but he should have thrown it in Orodruin's fire where it was made. For Isildur, and for all the others, the ring always promised more than it could deliver. In fact, Tolkien personifies the ring where it is ultimately seen as self-focused, manipulating those who possess it for its evil goals.

I hope that you see the connection. Idolatry is a disease that manifests itself outwardly, but is created inwardly. A. W. Tozer warns of this reality when he says, "An idol of the mind is as offensive to God as an idol of the hand."[1] Perhaps the reason that you are still struggling with idolatry is because it is in your heart, not your hand. You can forever destroy the visible idol that you hold most precious, but the memory of it can still control your daily life. Remember, the Israelites melted the golden calf, but the condition of their heart had not changed. Their idolatry was much deeper and would manifest itself in even greater ways later in their history.

In this chapter, my aim is to bring you face-to-face with the biblical diagnosis of idolatry, namely, your deceitful, depraved, sick, sinful heart. The question I am going to ask you to wrestle

1. Tozer, *The Knowledge of the Holy*, 8.

with and which follows from this diagnosis is, *why is the human heart quick to create, follow, and worship idols?* But before I answer this, allow me to address a few caveats regarding how our culture views your heart. Once I have burst some cultural bubbles, we will proceed and engage some key biblical texts regarding your heart and idolatry. These texts will provide the proof that idolatry is an internal reality.

Do Not Trust Your Heart

The life of a college pastor and now, a college professor, is quite interesting. I get the privilege of hearing people give some of the worst advice and counsel imaginable. The comments that are cringe-worthy always seem to occur in the context of romantic relationships, or the desire to have one. On more than one occasion, sitting in a group of well-intended young men seeking wisdom on which girl to date, I have heard the phrase uttered, "Just trust your heart." The words, even now, make my skin crawl. May I just say that this phrase is probably the poorest dating guidance in the history of mankind? No, brother, do not trust your heart, it will always lead you astray.

I am convinced that our postmodern Western culture values following what feels right over and against practical, common sense wisdom. Proverbs 19:21 reminds us that, "Many plans are in a man's heart, but the counsel of the Lord will stand." So, yes, there is wisdom in guarding your heart, but not in following it. Why is our Western culture enamored with the heart? The answer lies in postmodernism's deference to feelings over sound logic. You should face this reality now; how someone feels about a subject, sometimes even competing subjects that require them to accept contradictions in their worldview, is the new normal.

A postmodern feminist is applauded publicly for her admission before all that she has had an abortion. But the same person will fight for the rights of women who are trapped in modern day slavery. We, as Christians, would look at both of these situations and say that they are fundamentally about the same idea, the principle that life is precious. Nevertheless, the postmodernist vehemently argues that one is a choice and the other is a cause. Illogical hypocrisy runs deep in Western culture and it is a result of people placing feelings above facts. The heart is a mischievous false god.

One of the primary caveats regarding how our Western culture views the heart is that feelings are powerful influencers of behavior. One of the major principles in cognitive behavioral theory (CBT) is that thinking affects feelings and as a result, our behavior. In ministry, I have seen this pattern repeated over and over, primarily in the domain of marriage. Typically, when a couple comes to me as a pastor for marital counseling, they are already either in serious trouble or they are looking for evidence to support divorce. I often hear the phrase, "I feel like he/she just does not love me anymore."

Unraveling statements such as this one are difficult, but I always try to steer the couples away from their feelings and towards the truths revealed in Scripture about relationships. These times in marital conflict are critical. I wish I could tell you more success stories than failures, but the statistics just do not support such a reality. Feelings are powerful and once someone is led by their feelings, the train is speeding down the tracks too fast. Please do not misunderstand me. I am not saying you should never have feelings. I certainly am not advising you to harden your heart. What I am saying is do not be ruled by them. Our postmodern culture will always validate your feelings no matter how ridiculous they are. You must resist.

Staying with the illustration about marriage, my wife Stephanie and I will celebrate 22 years together on August 21. During our time with one another, there were, are, and prophetically will be many times where I love my wife, but I really do not like her. Relax ladies, the reverse of that statement is also true. A relationship that is based solely on the heart will inevitably end up in trouble. Listen, you will always discover the depth of your relationship with your spouse when you meet real adversity together. Your heart will not lead you to honor a marriage contract that has been broken, but the gospel will compel you to be faithful to the marriage covenant you established before God. Do not trust your heart. Trust the gospel.

The Deceitful, Sick Heart: Jeremiah 17

The ministry and life of the prophet Jeremiah may be summed up with two words, idolatry and judgment. Hafemann describes the ministry of Jeremiah with the following words, "The focus of Jeremiah's calling and subsequent ministry was on the divine judgment to be meted out in Israel's exile."[2] Thompson perhaps sums up the problems Jeremiah faced when he comments, "The greatest offense of all was the rejection of Yahweh himself as Israel's sovereign Lord. There could be no shared allegiance between Yahweh and any other god."[3] The test before this prophet was to address a pluralistic, syncretistic nation.

A particularly revealing indictment on the pollution that idolatry has caused in Israel is given in Jeremiah 3:2, "Lift up your eyes to the bare heights and see; where have you not been violated? You have polluted a land with your harlotry and with your wickedness." Later, Jeremiah 10:5 declares in a stinging satire on idolatry that idols are "like a scarecrow in a cucumber field. . .They must be carried because they cannot walk!" In one of the most shocking statements, God tells Jeremiah not to pray for the people of Israel and Judah for he is not going to listen when they pray because of their idolatrous ways. It is clear that God has had enough. Judgment is coming.

The root cause of their idolatry is revealed in Jeremiah 17:1–10. It is the heart. The prophet begins his lament on the heart by saying that the sin of God's people is written down with an iron stylus on their hearts. In other words, it is engraved permanently so that they will never forget what they have done before the Lord. The summary statement of Jeremiah's rebuke comes in 17:9, "The

---

2. Hafemann, "Paul's Jeremiah Ministry in Reverse," in *Paul's Message and Ministry in Covenant Perspective*, 110.

3. Thompson, *The Book of Jeremiah*, 8.

The Biblical Diagnosis of the Human Heart

heart is more deceitful than all else and is desperately sick; who can understand it?" The answer to his question is not left unanswered. It is the Lord who knows the hearts of men. The Lord God tests the hearts of humanity and gives to them according to their sinful, idolatrous ways.

The adjectives that Jeremiah uses to describe the human heart are significant. First, he says that the heart is *deceitful*. The Hebrew word here is also used for uneven ground that is difficult to travel. Thus, the idiom comes across as one who is uneven in their ways, unstable and difficult to predict. I think it is safe to say that this picture is a fairly accurate description of the heart. The path that your heart lays out before you may look safe and pleasing to the eye, but be assured, there is always trouble right around the corner. Your heart will lead you to believe that it has pure motives. In reality, it is deceiving you.

I like to run. Actually, let me be a little more accurate with that statement. I run so I can eat whatever I want. In my mind, the 5K and the box of Krispy Kreme donuts balance out on the scale of healthy living. My son Chase joins me and typically runs ahead of me instead of with me. Several years ago we were running some trails at Lake Lenexa in Kansas City. In typical fashion, Chase was ahead and I was struggling to keep up with him. Both of us had our headphones in and music blaring as motivation not to drop dead. As we came around a corner, I saw a Copperhead snake laying in the middle of the trail. Its head was raised in the air, scanning the air in every direction with his tongue. Chase did not see him.

I grabbed Chase's shirt and pulled hard on him to stop. He wheeled around and pulling his headphones out of his ears said to me, "What are you doing?!" Chase is an intense young man, which is why he is going to make a great Marine. I spun him around and pointed at the ground 6 feet away. His eyes widened and he immediately jumped behind me and said, "What are you going to do dad?" I knew exactly what to do. We gave the snake the trail and we went off into the woods.

Chase did not see the peril laying right in front of him on the trail. The road looked smooth, but he was just a few steps away from a deadly strike. Thankfully, I was there to stop him before he stepped on the snake. The human heart and its idolatrous bent will set you on a similar deceptive path like the one I just described. Just when you think you have hit your stride in life, the path becomes uneven and deceitfully deadly. Your idolatrous heart is no different than the people who Jeremiah spoke against on behalf of Yahweh. It will always lead you down a deceitful path of destruction.

Jeremiah not only pronounces the human heart as deceitful, but *desperately sick*. The New English Translation of the Bible gives the rendering that the heart is "incurable." The result of a heart that is deceitful above all else is an incurable sickness. The longer that a person is deceived by idolatry, the more sick they will become. Solomon shares a similar, honest diagnosis of the human heart when he says in Ecclesiastes 9:3 that, "The hearts of the sons of men are full of evil and insanity is in their hearts throughout their lives. Afterwards they go to the dead." Left unchecked, the idol production in your heart will end in sickness, insanity, and death.

I want to pause for a moment here with you. The objection might be, "That is a very hopeless picture of the human condition. You are being judgmental. After all, people are basically good at heart." No, that is wrong on all three accounts. The human condition is not hopeless, I have read the New Testament. I am not being judgmental, I am simply being biblical. If you have issues with what I am saying, do not argue with me, argue with the Bible. Finally, with a resounding and firm answer, people are not basically good, they are sinful. Put the book down and peruse Romans 3:9–20.

God used Jeremiah to press upon the condition of the human heart. The prophet reveals that their idolatry is the resultant behavior of a deceitful, sick heart. It is now important to further illuminate the condition of the human heart from a passage in the New Testament. While Jeremiah reveals the origins of an idolatrous heart, the Apostle Paul in Romans goes one step further by declaring its consequences.

The Biblical Diagnosis of the Human Heart

The Foolish, Depraved Heart: Romans 1

D. A. Carson remarks that, "No New Testament writer has provided a more profound, terrifying, and yet strangely compassionate account of the wrath of God than Paul in Romans 1:18–3:20."[4] Later, in further describing Romans 1, Carson notes, "God letting the nations go their own way sounds very much like God giving people up to their sinful ways."[5] The recipients of the letter of Romans seem to have much in common with the audience of Jeremiah. This observation is not coincidence for once again, the human heart is the culprit.

After Paul makes an argument from natural revelation for the existence and knowledge of God, he concedes in Romans 1:21 that although humanity knew God, "they became futile in their speculations and their foolish heart was darkened." He goes on to say that as fools, they exchanged God's glory for idols of their own creation. Their futile speculations and foolish heart has caused a darkness to settle over their understanding of God's true ways. Moo rightly says, "People who refuse to acknowledge God end up with minds that are 'disqualified' from being able to understand and acknowledge the will of God."[6]

God's consequent legal wrath against idolatrous humanity is fully explained by Paul with the phrase, "God gave them over," seen in Romans 1:24, 26, and 28. The consequences of an idolatrous heart are clearly stated. It appears that a depraved, sinful heart that is engaged in idolatrous practices will eventually arrive at the point where God says, "Okay, if you will not follow My ways, then have it your way."

The depiction of the things that God hands people over to is bleak. He gives them over to corporate impurity, degrading passions, and depraved thinking. In a stunning statement, Paul says that even though people know the indictment of God against such immoral behavior, they give hearty approval to those who

---

4. Carson, *The Gagging of God: Christianity Confronts Pluralism*, 233.
5. Ibid., 308.
6. Moo, *The Epistle to the Romans*, 118.

habitually practice these idolatrous ways. If you can imagine a crowd of people cheering over the sickest behavior imaginable, you are coming close to understanding the words of Paul in Romans 1.

Like Jeremiah, the words that Paul uses to describe the heart are key to grasping the perils of idolatry. First, he says that the heart is *foolish*. The adjective Paul uses is the same one used by Moses when he records God's prosecution of idolatrous Israel in Deuteronomy 32:21, "They have made Me jealous with what is not God; They have provoked Me to anger with their idols. So I will make them jealous with those who are not a people; I will provoke them to anger with a *foolish* nation." Hear me clearly on this principle, it is one thing to be ignorant, it is another thing altogether to be foolish.

I have done many things in life out of total ignorance. The crux of ignorance is action without understanding the consequences. Foolishness, on the other hand, recognizes the consequences, but chooses to act regardless of the penalty. As proof of this truth, I submit to you my freshman year of college. A word of advice, there is a direct correlation between going to class and passing a class. My first year of college was a total disaster. Believe me when I tell you, I was not ignorant, I was foolish. I knew fully well the consequences of my behavior, but I chose instead the path of party all night and sleep all day. One of the most shocking realities of idolatry is not when it is practiced in ignorance, but when it is embraced in foolishness.

Paul also labels the heart as *depraved*. What images come to mind when you hear of someone who is depraved? I am guessing that the one of the first images is that of a serial killer along the lines of Ted Bundy or Jeffrey Dahmer. You are much less likely to arrive at an image of your grandmother wearing her favorite apron and holding a warm plate of chocolate chip cookies. However, as the Bible makes clear, depravity is not limited to the most heinous acts. It is the condition of every human heart. Of course, the consequences of our actions are different, but the propensity for great evil and depravity is humanity's common denominator.

The Biblical Diagnosis of the Human Heart

This difficult truth regarding depravity is why we read story after story of people who we thought we knew being discovered as something or someone else. You always hear the phrase, "He was such a quiet, nice young man." He may be quiet and nice on the outside, but inside there might be a monster lurking in the shadows. The irony of idolatry lies in the production of depravity in our souls. The idol promises glorious things, but in truth, it produces inglorious ones. We look to idols for peace and the potential for a normal, sanitized, moral life. Instead, we discover the hollow god for what it is, an empty vessel that produces depravity which we hide because of a warped sense of shame.

I want to exhort you to come out of the shadows. Paul has already reminded you that your behavior is fully manifest before the God of the universe. The only way to be free of the hollow god of foolishness and depravity is to admit and repent of your sin. You may just find that you are not as alone as you think you are. The true prospect for a *good* life is not in service to a god of your own creation, but in submission to the God who made you. In the pages that follow, I am going to remind you that hope does exist for the one who desires to break free from the slavery of idolatry. If you are ready, you will find that the biblical diagnosis of the human heart is not left without a solution.

The New Heart: Ezekiel 36

The condemnation of idolatry spoken by Jeremiah is tempered, if not eclipsed, by the possibility of a prophetic fulfillment revealed in Ezekiel 36. The context of this major Old Testament prophet is more than likely contemporaneous with that of Jeremiah. But, where Jeremiah strikes a tone of wrath against idolatry, Ezekiel is given a message of freedom from idolatry. This liberty, however, will not be found in a renewed human commitment to the old covenant written on tablets of stone.

Early in Ezekiel's prophecy we get the idea that God's people are in trouble. God says through the prophet in 6:5, "I will also lay the dead bodies of the sons of Israel in front of their idols; and

I will scatter your bones around your altars." Texts like this one sound like a script from a lost Wes Craven horror movie. And if you think it could not get worse, read Ezekiel 9 and the vision of the slaughter of Jerusalem. When Yahweh utters phrases like the one in Ezekiel 9:10, "I will bring their conduct upon their heads," you can certain He is not being metaphorical or cute. Nor is He just in a bad mood. God is a just judge.

It takes thirty five chapters for light to break in upon the dark picture given to Ezekiel. Chapter 36 begins a series of promises that include God cleansing the people of Israel from all of their idols. Once this is done, the Lord declares a magnificent new reality in verses 26–27.

> Moreover, I will give you a new heart and put a new spirit within you; and I will remove the heart of stone from your flesh and give you a heart of flesh. I will put my Spirit within you and cause you to walk in My statutes, and you will be careful to observe my ordinances."

I want you to notice two important truths from this text in Ezekiel. The first is the *method* through which this promise comes to the people of God. Go back and read these verses one more time. Now, did you pick up on the amount of first person pronouns in the passage? Count how many times that God says, "I will." In the span of a few verses that round out this beautiful chapter in Ezekiel, God says an incredible fifteen times, "I will." This type of language makes the final verse of the chapter leap off of the page, "Then they will know that I am the Lord." The only method for curing an idolatrous heart that will be successful is the action of the Lord. As verse 32 reminds us, God does this not for our sake.

You do not have the tools available to fix the problem of idolatry that has infected your heart. Even if you destroy an idol, I guarantee that another one will quickly take its place. I will be so bold as to say this in a different way. The successful purging of idolatry from your heart is a useless exercise apart from total divine intervention. Think about this illustration. Suppose you decide to try skydiving with your wife for your anniversary. On the way to airfield you get into a fight. As you walk to the plane,

The Biblical Diagnosis of the Human Heart

she glares at you with that stare. The skydiving instructor greets you, telling you that he is going to pack your parachute first. At that point, your wife raises her hand and says, "Would you mind if I packed his parachute?"

I do not care how much I love or trust my wife, but in that scenario, I am never allowing my wife to touch my parachute. For starters, she knows nothing about packing a parachute safely. Secondly, we just had a major fight. Third, we have really good life insurance policies. Of course, I am only exaggerating, my wife would never kill me. The illustration is imperfect, but I am always going to trust the person with the most expertise. This is why I will never let my dentist, even though he is a doctor, operate on my knee. May I just submit, then, how much more the problem of idolatry? God is the only viable method.

The second truth you should observe from this text is the *means* by which God will accomplish this permanent transformation. This promised change will be effected through the indwelling presence of the Holy Spirit. The text draws a straight line between the presence of the Spirit of God and the ability for God's people to be caused to walk in His ways. It is apparent that the Holy Spirit is able to produce covenant faithfulness in hearts that once obeyed idols. This assurance from God is good news. It means that God is not going to use a new program to fix your idolatrous heart, He is going to use the third Person of the Trinity, the Holy Spirit.

Ezekiel's prophetic echoes find their fulfillment in Paul's words to the idolatrous Christians at Corinth. Paul says in 2 Corinthians 3:3 that this church is a letter of Christ, "written not with ink, but with the Spirit of the living God, not on tablets of stone but on tablets of human hearts." The English translation of the last phrase does not do the text justice. Paul literally says, "Not on plates of stone, but fleshy heart plates." Just a few chapters later in 2 Corinthians 5:17, he reveals an implausible truth, "Therefore if anyone is in Christ, he is a new creature; the old things passed away; behold, new things have come."

Lately, I have found the wonder that is known as Gorilla glue. Just in the last few weeks, I have put back together a baby gate, a lamp, and a candelabra. This product is amazing, yet it only provides a temporary sense of security. I am, at best, cautiously optimistic about the integrity of the household items I just listed. God is not doing minor repair work on your heart with His cosmic bottle of glue. No, the Bible declares that you are something brand new. There is no need to be skeptical about whether or not your new heart will succeed where your old one failed. God is not providing a temporary security from the disease of idolatry, He has already given you an eternal one. I understand at this juncture if you are unsure about the biblical truths laid out in the chapter. If so, sit back and let me tell you the story of a man named Rick.

The Story of Rick

I still remember the first time I saw Rick driving around the small town where I served as a pastor. He was driving a rusty, beat up Ford truck and pulling a flatbed trailer full of junk. Both looked like they were about ready to fall apart. His hair was not combed and his beard looked like it had small animals for residents. His dark eyes communicated the message, "Get out of my way or I will hurt you." When I encountered him at the grocery store, my polite, pastoral greetings would be met with cold stares.

Little did Rick know, but we were praying for him as a church family. His wife, Diane, started coming to church not long after we moved to the community. During prayer times, she would pour out her heart for her husband, begging us to pray for his salvation. On several occasions, she came directly to the door of the parsonage with tears in her eyes. I am not sure if there has ever been a man that I prayed more fervently for than Rick. For seven years we prayed as church family with no results. Rick remained unchanged and unaffected.

A year after we moved to Kansas City, I returned to preach a funeral service at the church. I walked into the sanctuary and, as customary, began to greet people. Scanning the room, my eyes stopped at a guy that looked like Rick. For a moment I thought I was mistaken, that is, until Rick caught my eyes and hurriedly ran

The Biblical Diagnosis of the Human Heart

up to me. I put my hand out to shake his hand, but he was having none of that sort of formal greeting. He grabbed me and embraced me with the biggest smile on his face. His hair was combed and beard trimmed.

Once the initial shock wore off, Rick began to tell me his testimony. I didn't even have to ask him what had happened, he was eager. He shared about his heart attack and time spent in the hospital. He told me that it was in the ICU that he knew his life was about to change. It was in that hospital bed that he had given his life to Jesus. Rick was a visual portrait of a new creature. The old things were passed away, new things had come. I am telling you, he was not only new on the outside, but he looked brand new on the outside. It was like Gollum had transformed back into Sméagol.

The truth is that Rick and many others like him have bought into the postmodern lie of following your heart. The outcome is deception and darkness, a perpetual cycle of enslavement to sin through a gruesome idol that shows no compassion or mercy. The question for you is; in what areas of life is your heart deceiving you? Yes, you are a new creation and the Bible promises that the Spirit has sealed your heart until the day of redemption. But, your heart is still sinful and capable of leading you where you should not go. May I encourage you to rely on the Lord with *all* your heart? Resist the descent into the idols created by your heart. Lean upon the wisdom of the Lord and not the distorted feelings of your heart. Please, do not trust your heart. Trust the Lord.

5

The Biblical Reality of Spiritual Warfare

You are at War!

SINCE THE END OF World War II, there have been fifteen major global conflicts. It appears that our world is well acquainted with war. I would offer for your consideration a more sobering reality. You are at war with idols all around you. The truth is that you are, right now, fighting a spiritual battle with idolatry. Please allow me to make an important prediction. You can win the battle and ultimately, the war that idols rage against your soul. The barometer for you to assess the state of the war begins with admitting that you are at war.

I want you to reflect for a moment on the following question; why is humanity losing the war with idolatry? The answer I am going to offer you in this chapter may surprise you. I will attempt to prove to you that humanity is supernaturally deceived, unaware that they are even engaged in a battle with idols. In the words of their affectionate Uncle Screwtape, "It is funny how mortals always

The Biblical Reality of Spiritual Warfare

picture us as putting things into their minds: in reality our best work is done by keeping things out."[1] Friends, you are at war.

This chapter will proceed to offer for you a biblical solution through an important text on idolatry, 2 Corinthians 10:1–6. Before we go any further, I want you to do three things. First, take a few minutes and read this important passage. Second, put the book down and pray. The startling reality is that I am asking to pick up your weapon as you read this chapter. A sobering truth is that many of you will shoulder your weapon, believing that the battle really is not that serious. You need to pray. Finally, find a place where you will not be distracted. The idols in your life do not want you placing God's truth in your mind and heart. Remember, you are at war.

Stranger Things: Supernatural Deception

I am always looking for a new show to binge watch on Netflix. The most recent in my playlist was a series specifically produced by Netflix called *Stranger Things*. There were three hooks that sunk deep into me and scratched the entertainment itch. One, of course, was that the series was set in the 1980's. Next was the opening scene where the main characters were sitting in their basement playing board games. Finally, I loved the plot of this young group of kids solving a supernatural mystery, battling things that are unseen.

Without giving away the entire plot, the show is designed around a group of young boys searching for their friend who went missing after a heated game of Dungeons & Dragons. As they hunt, they find a young girl with supernatural gifts. Eventually, they uncover a conspiracy in their small town involving a local government facility. All I can tell you is that along the way, their eyes are opened to a different world than the one in which they live. They are challenged and forced to accept a new supernatural reality.

1. Lewis, *The Screwtape Letters*, 16.

Maybe I have a future as an abstract marketing writer for Netflix. The fact is, I enjoy shows that work with new ideas instead of resurrecting old ones. If Hollywood decides to do a reboot of Gilligan's Island, I am filing a petition. The reason this series works so well is because it creates tension for the characters. This pressure they feel is a direct result of their worldview being challenged by the supernatural force breaking into their lives. In order to fight and defeat this new opponent, they have to come to grips with the fact that it even exists.

You cannot defeat an interdimensional being if you do not believe in alternative realities where faceless interdimensional beings reside and attempt to turn you into a cocoon host for their interdimensional offspring. Okay, I have said too much. May I suggest to you that you face a much more frightening opponent than anything you will find on streaming TV services? Ephesians 6:12 reminds us that, "our struggle is not against flesh and blood, but against the rulers, against the powers, against the world forces of this darkness, against the spiritual forces of wickedness in the heavenly places." Did you catch that description? You are engaged in a supernatural war that is being fought for the souls of humanity. The primary tool of the enemy you fight against is deception. You need to expand your supernatural worldview.

The experience of a majority of Christians is an implausible denial of spiritual warfare against idolatry. I see two possibilities for why our fellow church members disavow this biblical reality. First, it is probable that a person might be distinctively Christian, culturally unengaged, and spiritually ignorant. The second is that an individual could be distinctively postmodern, culturally Christian, and spiritually isolated. Before I explain what I mean, let me comment that both groups are somewhat of a generalization. Nevertheless, that does not imply that they are not accurate categories for which our church members might fall into regarding the rejection of idolatrous warfare.

The latter group I just described walks the halls of your local church with their four inch thick study Bible signed by their favorite pastor. They can quote the latest podcast or blog of the most

The Biblical Reality of Spiritual Warfare

popular American pontificators. They have made the pilgrimage to the Creation museum in Kentucky and the closest they have ever come to cultural engagement is a tattoo of a Greek or Hebrew word on their arm. They are distinctively Christian in their identity, but so culturally unengaged that they would not recognize an idol even if it announced its arrival through an alliterated three point message and an illustration about an ancient hymn writer. If you were to ask them about spiritual warfare, their response might be, "Oh yeah, I did the Beth Moore study back in 2008."

For the record, lest I offend my brothers and sisters in Christ, I love study Bibles, podcasts, blogs, the Creation museum, biblical tattoos, alliterated sermons, and Beth Moore. What I cannot stomach is a Christian that is self-deceived in their praxiology and anemic in the reality of the cultural battles we face against idolatry. It makes little sense to sit on the deck of an aircraft carrier and read a book about the benefits of a cruise ship. No, if you are at war, you fight. It is time for our brothers and sisters in Christ who are spiritually ignorant to wake up and embrace a wartime footing.

The second group I described also inhabits your local community of believers. They are so enamored with making Christianity culturally relevant and cool that they have lost any sort of distinctiveness. James 4:4 puts it clearly, "You adulteresses, do you not know that friendship with the world is hostility toward God? Therefore, whoever wishes to be a friend of the world makes himself an enemy of God." Jesus said it best when he warns the disciples in Matthew 10:16 before He sends them out on mission to their culture, "Behold, I send you out as sheep in the midst of wolves." You can trust Jesus. Remember, He always tells the truth.

Such Christians, and I use that term rather broadly here, are functionally postmodern. They have isolated themselves from the truth of God's word in favor of the latest cultural brand of evangelicalism. They are postmodern in their identity and so culturally engaged that their idols are baptized and integrated as harmless additions to the ecclesiastical community. The justification of their inclusion colludes with the perilous idol of remaining relevant. Pastor, if you are tempted to open your Christmas Eve service with a smoke machine and a Snoop Dog rap, then please check yourself before you wreck yourself.

Your worldview regarding spiritual warfare needs to radically change. The problem is that you live in a postmodern culture that denies the objective reality of this campaign. In order for you to arrive at a place where you are distinctively Christian, culturally engaged, and spiritually prepared, you must understand how the pillar of postmodernism knowledge integrates with biblical spiritual warfare.

Postmodernism and Spiritual Warfare

Postmodernism's view on knowledge is grounded in an inconsistent skepticism of anything that is declared objectively true. For this reason, it is no surprise that they struggle with the reality of spiritual warfare. To be fair, a postmodern thinker would validate your claim of experiencing spiritual warfare. However, if you would draw a connection for them from your experience to the truth of Scripture, then the hand of protest gets raised. The experience of spiritual warfare for a postmodernist might be real, but its source is inside of man, not outside of him.

It is beyond doubt that our Western culture is fascinated, possibly obsessed, with experiences surrounding spiritual warfare. Every year the cinematic smorgasbord is increasingly saturated with movies that focus on the demonic. Just this year alone there are opportunities for you to visually experience dead children being brought back to life through ancient rituals, a possession of two sisters in England, a boy whose nightmares become reality, and even the demons of an ancient Japanese forest where people go to commit suicide. Several of these stories are touted as having a basis in real events. Apparently, the elite Hollywood directors have not caught up to the postmodern disbelief in objective truth.

I have personally, one two occasions, encountered people who I believe were demon possessed. One was a young man who foamed at the mouth and growled at me while I shared the gospel with him. No, this event did not happen while in some third world

The Biblical Reality of Spiritual Warfare

country. It occurred on the streets of Olathe, Kansas. Now, I could have concluded that this young man had some mental illness which perpetuated his irrational and disturbing behavior. Maybe he was not taking his medicine. Perhaps he put on a show for me, trying to scare me with an unchecked manifestation of anger rooted in some traumatic childhood experience. Or, could it be that the best explanation is the one found in the Christian worldview?

A postmodernist would not refute the experience that I had, but the explanation for it stops there and goes no further. I apologize, but that is nonsense. It is at times like these that the truth of Scripture becomes illuminated and clear. I did not find myself at that point quoting The Exorcist, "The power of Christ compels you!" but 1 John 4:4, "Greater is He who is in you than He who is in the world." When the objective truth of the Bible matches up with our experiences, postmodernism begins to show the cracks in its foundation and the structure begins to crumble.

Whether a postmodern thinker will admit it or not, there is a grand narrative that exists in the universe. It is one that originates in the truth claims about spiritual warfare found in the pages of the Bible. The false god of your feelings will always betray you. Remember, there will be days where you do not want to feel that spiritual warfare is true or real, but it is and you are at war. As Christians living in a pluralistic culture, it is critical that we point those around us to the objective evidence of spiritual warfare. We must live in such a way that our lives reflect the struggle against evil that wishes to dominate and rule our lives.

You may ask at this point, "What could I possibly do that will bear witness to the reality of spiritual warfare?" That is a great question. It is going to primarily involve you tearing down some idols that have strategically placed themselves in and over your life. You are going to need a strategy to fight a lifetime campaign against idolatry. You must realize that the weapons in your arsenal will never be found in the fleshly realm of this world. How can I say these things with such confidence? It is because I have read 2 Corinthians 10:1–6.

Tearing Down Idols: 2 Corinthians 10:1–6

I have spent a majority of my academic life over the past six years researching and writing on the letter of 2 Corinthians. From the beginning, my pursuit of a PhD in Biblical Studies was intertwined with this wonderful and challenging Pauline letter. More than a few people pursue the elusive dissertation, resulting in years of anguish over what area they might make a scholarly contribution. Not me, I spread my pain out over the entire scope of the doctoral journey.

I became convinced from an early point in my research that the passage of 2 Corinthians 10:1–6 is one of the most exegetically abused texts in the Bible. Popular preaching on this text often focuses correctly on spiritual warfare, but wrongly interprets the type of warfare Paul is describing for this church. The warfare that the modern pastor refers to is one that occurs in the context of individualistic mental battles that amount to nothing more than a vain attempt at taking every sinful thought that I have captive. Supposing I could predict my sinful thoughts, what would I do if I ever caught one? Should I put them in some spiritual holding cell? If so, what if the grid fails and they all get out again?

Of course, I am speaking with a twinge of sarcasm. Nevertheless, the logical outcomes of reducing 2 Corinthians 10:1–6 to this interpretation do create more confusion than answers for the average Christian. It is true that 2 Corinthians has presented numerous challenges for scholars with respect to understanding Paul's arguments in the letter. Just flip through a critical commentary on the epistle and you will understand exactly what I mean. Theories about multiple authorship and partitioned correspondence abound. I will spare you the technical arguments regarding these and defer instead to what we do know from the letter.

The background and context of 2 Corinthians is not difficult to establish. We know that Paul wrote to a church plagued by divisions, caused by both internal and external factors. The internal influences which resulted in a divided body of believers were boasting, sexual immorality, lawsuits, marital issues, abuse

The Biblical Reality of Spiritual Warfare

of Christian liberty, misuse of spiritual gifts, and the denial of a bodily resurrection of the saints. All of these concerns may be summarized under the heading of a misunderstanding of the Lorship of Jesus Christ. And you think your church has problems?

The external features of the Corinthian divisiveness were much more serious. This threat endangered the foundations of Paul's ministry and the survival of the church at Corinth. Paul describes this external menace in 2 Corinthians 11:3 as men who were, "False apostles, deceitful workers, disguising themselves as apostles of Christ." Furthermore, Paul tells us that the church was in danger of being led astray from the truth of the gospel by these men who were preaching another Jesus, one of a completely different kind. What was the main cause for this church's susceptibility towards false teaching? At the root of everything, once again, was idolatry.

In one of the best books on this letter and the context of the city, Savage says that, "In Corinth, perhaps more than elsewhere, people looked to the cults for satisfaction, and satisfaction as they defined it, as personal exultation and glory."[2] The essence of his argument here is that the Corinthians wanted their religion to gratify them, not to transform their lives. Does that sound familiar to you? It is just as likely that the same description could apply to our Western postmodern culture. Folks, idolatry is not a new phenomenon.

Second Corinthians 10:3–5 rests at the core of Paul's argument for a solution to the idolatry manifesting itself in the church. Prior to this passage, the apostle pleads for his readers to consider his authority, not as someone who wants to be bold towards them, but instead as an example of Jesus. Paul proposes that he is going to be courageously bold in the exercising of judgment against the false teachers in the church. They attack Paul's appearance in the flesh, but Paul reminds his readers they do not wage a campaign in the flesh.

Paul warns that his visit to Corinth will bring about the destruction of idolatrous speculations, which are understood

---

2. Savage, *Power through Weakness*, 52.

through the metaphor in 10:5, "every lofty thing raised up against the knowledge of God." By the way, the word he uses for "lofty thing" is the same word used in the Old Testament historical books of 1 and 2 Kings for the high places that Solomon built while waiting for the temple to be constructed. For instance, we read in 1 Kings 3:2 that, "The people were offering sacrifices at the high places." We are told just a few verses later that Solomon, "would offer up a thousand burnt sacrifices on the altar there."

Initially, it would appear that the people were sacrificing at the high places due to the practical demands of a nonexistent temple, that is, until we read in 1 Kings 11:7, "Then Solomon built a high place for Chemosh, the false god of Moab." Solomon's enticement to marry foreign women resulted in Israel's worship of the false gods Chemosh, Ashtoreth, and Molech. I believe that Paul is possibly alluding to the high places of Israel's idolatry so that his readers will understand the serious nature of their problem. Some might say, "But I thought Paul's readers were Corinthians (Gentiles), not Jews?"

This question is appropriate and true to some extent. I would argue that Paul writes to a diverse audience of both Jews and Gentiles using a mixed metaphor. While the Jews at Corinth might hear the echoes of their idolatrous history, the Gentiles would surely have to look no further than a massive geological formation on the horizon of their city. Corinth's military strength was located in its acropolis, situated approximately 5 miles (8 km) to the south of port of Lechaion. Known simply as the Acrocorinth, this outcropping of stone stood a towering 1,880 feet (573 m) above the city, proving to be a key position against any enemy who would come by land or sea.

By the mid-first century of Paul's day, Corinth not only exemplified ethnic diversity, but also religious pluralism as well. Archaeological evidence has revealed temples dedicated to various Greek deities including Apollo, Aphrodite, Demeter, Hermes, Persephone, Poseidon, and numerous others.[3] Additionally, a

---

3. Bookidis and Stroud, *Demeter and Persephone at Corinth*.

The Biblical Reality of Spiritual Warfare

temple to the famed Egyptian goddess Isis was prevalent.[4] Morever, by this period the emperor cult may have been in existence and influential in the city.[5] Finally, the presence of Jewish practice was not excluded as attested by a marble inscription found on the Acrocorinth.[6]

You can now begin to see why Paul talks not only about taking every thought captive, but also the use of spiritual weapons for the "destruction of fortresses." I do not have the space here to recount for you the rest of Corinth's history. It would be worth your time to research what happened to Corinth in BC 146. Let's just say the result of their disobedience to Rome resulted in the destruction of the idolatrous temples at the Corinthian high place called the Acrocorinth. This idolatrous history surrounding the city surely influenced Paul's exhortations regarding the situation in the church.

The connection with postmodern idolatry and the answers Paul offers to the Corinthians regarding idolatry are not difficult to grasp. Spiritual blindness to the slavery that idols hold over our lives is a common point of contact with all of humanity throughout all of history. The first century Christians are no different in their spiritual struggle than Christians living in a pluralistic, postmodern culture. Everyone is an idolater. As a result, passages like 2 Corinthians 10:1–6 must not be appropriated by pastors or teachers as individualized spiritual warfare against subjective sin. This text is not about changing your sinful behavior so you can feel good about your moral standing before a holy God. It is addressing the danger that the church faces in their corporate war against idolatrous false teachers.

The metaphors that Paul uses in this passages provide a rhetorical nudge for his readers to consider and decide which side they will join in the campaign, that is, on the side of Paul's divinely

---

4. Bricault and Veymiers, "Isis in Corinth: The Numismatic Evidence, City, Image, and Religion," 392–416.

5. Camia and Kantiréa, "The Imperial Cult in the Peloponnese," 375–406.

6. Horsley, *New Documents Illustrating Early Christianity: A Review of the Greek Inscriptions and Papyri Published in 1979*, 213.

appointed ministry or the super-apostles fleshly created idolatry. Because these church members are following idolatry, Paul warns against judgment before the bench of God. We can learn, in our Western culture that the same exhortations hold true. You must choose sides and avoid the lie of neutrality in the war against idolatry. If you elect to fight, you will find that you are not alone in your struggle. On the other hand, if you avoid the conflict and remain numb to your idolatrous ways, then you must be aware that judgment is waiting for the proper time.

Grandpa Turner's Army Hat

I revealed earlier that my paternal grandfather, Carl Turner, landed at Normandy and spent his days in France. He passed away in 2003. I wish you could have met this man. He was one of the most gentle, loving, compassionate men I have ever known. He had a quiet demeanor, but you knew that underneath everything was a firm conviction of his beliefs. The man I called my grandfather was known to take out his false teeth and eat a spoonful of peanut butter in order to make us laugh.

Whenever I would ask him what he did in the Army, he would simply respond, "I was a cook." He would not talk much, if at all, about the war and his time fighting the Nazi regime. I still have a lapel pin that he pulled off the body of a Nazi officer. He never told me how it came to be in his possession. I was afraid to ask. We always knew that grandpa did more in the war than just "cook," but the stories were never told. He preferred instead to lead us as a family to know the Lord in the present rather than reminisce about battles fought in the past.

After his death, my dad and his sisters had an opportunity to go through some old boxes in the back of grandpa's closet. There in an old worn down box they found some pictures and a standard issue U.S. Army hat, circa 1940. One of the pictures was of my grandfather and some of his fellow soldiers in the forests of France. The snapshot looks like a scene from *The Dirty Dozen*. The most interesting thing was what they found in the hat. In a zipper

The Biblical Reality of Spiritual Warfare

pocket, my dad and his sisters discovered my grandfather's WWII medals. He had hidden them there for over sixty years. We do not know the reasons why he received the medals. All we know is that he fought well and did not give up until victory was achieved.

The point I want to make for you regarding spiritual warfare is simple. Like my grandfather, you can walk in integrity as a Christian, yet still wage war against a merciless enemy. It does not have to be a choice between pacifism and militarism in the war on idolatry. When it is time to fight, you must not hesitate. The battles that you win do not need medals of commendation for display. Let them develop your character and resolve for future challenges that you will face. Fight for your family, the church and the survival of its members. Resolve to pick up your spiritual weapons and stop fighting in the flesh. You are at war. You must embrace a wartime footing.

Biblical Solutions and Application

This chapter has sought to make you think about the reality of spiritual warfare against idolatry. I have attempted to prepare you to not only accept this reality, but also to consider the importance of engaging in the spiritual battles against the idols in your life. I challenged you to wrestle with the question of why humanity is losing the war with idolatry. We saw together the truth that our postmodern culture is supernaturally deceived, blissfully unaware that they are at war. Their penchant for subjective experiences divorced from objective truth has shoved them violently down a path of skeptical ignorance. What are the biblical solutions and applications to your life and the church? There are several that are worth mentioning.

First, and as obvious as it sounds, *spiritual warfare is real*. It matters little whether or not you have had a subjective experience of spiritual warfare to validate your feelings on the subject. I pray that this reality does not produce fear in your heart, but instead a firm resolve in your walk with Christ. The words of 1 Peter 5:8 should never become dull in your mind and heart, "Be of sober spirit, be on the alert. Your adversary, the devil, prowls around like a roaring lion, seeking someone to devour." These are not some words in a fantasy novel filled with mythical creatures. They reflect the objective reality of what you face each day.

Second, *spiritual warfare must be waged corporately*. In other words, you are never, if possible, to engage the enemy alone. The days of modeling our Christian combat after the likes of Rooster Cogburn, Rambo, or Jason Bourne must come to an end. I included three different eras here so you would get the illustration. Aside from the obvious fact that no one goes into modern or ancient warfare alone, we have the wonderful presence of first person plural pronouns in the text of 2 Corinthians 10:3–5. Just read the passage again and underline or circle the words "we" or "our" and you will get my argument.

Allow me to ask a simple question of you and then a very difficult one. The simple one is this: is it easier for you to fight a spiritual battle against idols by yourself or with others at your side? Now, hear the harder one: why are you still fighting alone? I have not read your personal journals but I bet the answer has something to do with shame and guilt. You are afraid of revealing your idols and the sin that they are keeping you enslaved to day after day. The lie of idolatry is that your sin master is unique. We are all broken. We are all sinners. It is time to set aside your pride and get transparently honest about the battle. I will wager that you will discover that you are not as alone as your think you are.

Finally, *victory in spiritual warfare is achievable in the present.* Here is another way of saying this; you can smash your idols and resist the temptation to glue them back together. Many Christians understand and long for the eschatological deliverance from the sin of this present world. We know that heaven will be absent of all of the pain and mess that our idols have created. In truth, it is a good thing that we possess this firm belief in what eternity holds for those who hope in Jesus. But let me encourage you, abiding in Jesus is not just an eternal reality, it should be a present experience. This promise is found when you acknowledge spiritual warfare and you start fighting alongside people who will lovingly and unashamedly hold you accountable for the sake of the gospel. Remember, you (all) are at war.

6

The Biblical Description of a Fallen World

The World is Broken

IN MY OPINION, THE strength of the evidence that our world is broken is directly proportional to the numbers of times a person has visited Wal Mart after 10:00 PM. There are just some things that I wish could be wiped clean from my memory. Case in point, I stood in line with a young lady once who was clearly under the influence of drugs. She asked me to help her hide from a stalker a few feet away as she jumped behind a rack of potato chips. I resisted the urge to say, "If he is stalking you, then what does that say about him?" I gladly played along with her. People who are high on drugs typically do not understand sarcasm.

A broken world is a perfect environment for idols to not only exist, but thrive. I believe there is a direct correlation between the overt presence of idolatry and a lack of a clear gospel witness. The places in the world where the gospel has not saturated the culture are environments where idols can boldly and openly walk without fear of reprisal. In places where the gospel is prevalent, idols often

The Biblical Description of a Fallen World

go underground. They hide in secrecy and their strategy is one of infiltration, rather than open attack. This latter reality is exactly where we stand in a secularized, postmodern culture.

This chapter will provide for you a primary theological reason for the ongoing problem of idolatry, namely, a fallen world. I plan to stitch together for you the doctrinal realities found in Genesis 3 as they are expressed through 1 John 2:15–17. These passages reveal the problem raised by idolatry in a postmodern context, that is, why idolatry is so prevalent, yet ignored by a majority of Christians in Western culture. The response is found in the truth that the idols within our postmodern culture are relativized and sanitized for your consumption.

A Ministry of Death

As if you needed more evidence that the world is broken, allow me to offer up a brief account of my final months as a small town pastor. To be completely honest, I struggled with the choice of narrating these events for you. Even after seven years, the pain is still very real. My story begins with a young man named Stoney Mack. In the summer prior to our departure, this young man gave his life to Jesus at church camp. The change in him was incredible. Six months later he would meet Jesus face to face.

Stoney and my oldest son Chase were best friends. And, in some ways, Stoney was like having another son. They spent a lot of time together as ten year old boys riding bicycles and having sleep overs. On New Year's Eve that year, Stoney had invited Chase to spend the night at his grandma's house with another friend Daniel. Chase begged me to go, but I said no. I wanted Chase to be home with his family. To this day, I still do not know the reason I refused, but I do know that it spared his life.

That night a fire broke out in the house, trapping the boys along with Stoney's older sister, her boyfriend, and their newborn baby. I will never forget hearing the phone ring on New Year's Day and receiving the news. Even now, writing this for you, I am holding back tears. I vividly remember telling my son that his best friend was gone. Our world is broken. There are some things I wish could be wiped from my memory. Five people perished that night in a tragic way, yet the tragedies were not finished.

The funerals were all held together at the school gymnasium. I was asked to officiate and bring the message. I struggled for days with what to say to a community that had been shaken to its core. There was no logical explanation for what had happened, so I found the courage to say these words, "Sin has caused our world to be broken. If there is no sin, there is no cross; no cross, no tomb; no tomb, no empty tomb; and if there is no empty tomb, there is no hope." What else could I do but offer the hope and promise that Jesus will one day make all things new? I rejoice that one day Chase and I will see Stoney Mack, Daniel, and many others we have lost through the brokenness of this world.

Just when I was about to catch my breath, the funerals began to pour in like a tidal wave. Some were for elderly people inside and outside our community. Perhaps one of the hardest was a funeral I officiated for a twelve year old young man who took his own life. From New Year's Day to the middle of March, I lost count of how many funerals I preached. I believe the number was in the low twenties. All I know is that it began with tragic loss and ended in the same way. That spring, we lost one of the patriarchs of our church in a car fire.

Charles was a WWII veteran who fought in the South Pacific. He had been a school teacher in St. Louis and retired in our small community. He and his wife had seen their dream come true of building a log cabin in the country. Some of our most treasured memories as a family were dinners with Charles and Maxine on their farm. We had a great relationship, mainly because they were true Cardinals fans in the midst of hostile KC Royals territory. Charles was a faithful pillar in our church.

The phone call I received about Charles from one our deacons was straight to the point, "Charles died in his car." My first thought was that Charles died of a heart attack or stroke while driving. After all, he was in his 80's. I was not prepared for the fact that his car had caught on fire while he was burning trash near his house. Our world is broken. There are some things that I wish could be wiped from my memory. It began to be apparent that my calling was rapidly becoming centered on death and grief. My final months as a pastor of a small town were affected deeply by the sting of death. Did I mention that our world is broken?

Idolatry is as Old as Genesis 3

Romans 8:20 reminds us that, "The creation was subjected to futility, not willingly, but because of him who subjected it." Paul can make this definitive statement because he has read Genesis 3. Just imagine for a moment being able to witness this incredible turning point in the history of humanity. We never fully comprehend the far reaching consequences of our choices. I often wonder if Adam and Eve understood that their rebellious decision would not only affect them, but also the *entire* created order.

Every semester here at Hannibal LaGrange University I have the opportunity to teach a five week session on Christian worldview to our incoming freshman class. One of my favorite questions to ask is why Paul says in Romans 5:12, "Through one man sin entered the world, and death through sin, and so death spread to all men." My inquiry for them is why the text does not say that through one *woman*, sin entered the world. After all, was it not Eve's fault that she took the fruit from the tree? The look of confusion on their faces is priceless.

This theological bubble gets burst when I take them to Genesis 3:6 and we actually read the passage. It is truly amazing the truths you discover when you pick up the Bible and read it. The text says, "She took from its fruit and ate; and she gave also to her husband with her." Did you catch the point? The Bible says that Adam was *with* Eve the entire time she is talking to Satan personified as a serpent. Friends, he was standing right by her side and he said not one word of protest. The theological description for this event is the silence of Adam. He abrogated his divinely given responsibility to cultivate, keep, and protect (Genesis 2:15–16).

Imagine how different life would have been if Adam turned to Eve and said, "Honey, I don't think it is a good idea to talk to snakes." Or, he could have lopped its head off with a machete. But, to be fair, he was naked and there was no place to keep one. The first sin in the Garden of Eden amounted to idolatry. Remember, an idol is anything visible or invisible that takes the place of God. So, for Adam and Eve, their sin was idolatrous. The desire to be like God, knowing good and evil, fueled by pride took the place of what God was already providing for them in a direct, personal, intimate relationship. The Enemy introduced them to the idol of pride and together, they ushered in a new fallen reality, and as a result, a fallen world.

Now, not only is humanity broken by sin, but so is the creation in which they reside. Yahweh says to Adam in Genesis 3:17a, "Cursed is the ground because of you; in toil you will eat of it all the days of your life." Ross reminds us, "The original sin of Adam and Eve brought into the race the conflict between good and evil, with the consequent painful toil, hardship, alienation, and death."[1] Waltke rightly notes, "The ecology of the earth is partly dependent on human morality."[2] As God is pronouncing judgment to Noah, he declares destruction upon all of creation, saying, "I am sorry that I have made *them*."[3] I imagine that the dolphin seated in the back of the meeting was tempted to raise a flipper in disapproval.

The effect of Adam's sin is comprehensive, regardless of guilt or innocence of any parties that are involved. In other words, the marring of creation by sin may be chalked up to collateral damage. This is why I cringe when I hear prosperity gospel televangelists proclaim that the latest natural disaster to strike America is God's judgment upon our sinful Western culture. It is in the realm of

---

1. Ross, *Creation and Blessing: A Guide to the Study and Exposition of Genesis*, 148.

2. Waltke, *Genesis: A Commentary*, 95.

3. Genesis 6:7.

The Biblical Description of a Fallen World

possibilities, but we do not know for sure. The more likely reason these tragedies occur is due to the creation groaning and suffering under the weight of sin. Our world is broken, but it will not be broken forever.

The truth is that humanity and creation will one day be set free from its slavery to corruption. Another favorite question I like to ask of my students is this one; will Christians live forever in heaven with Jesus? The room is often silent as they contemplate whether or not I am trying to trick them. In case you are wondering, it is a trick question. Christians will not live forever in heaven with Jesus. They will live forever in a new heavens and new *earth*. Take a minute and look up Revelation 21. Yes friends, we will all be new earth city dwellers.

It is no surprise that since idolatry was the primary cause of the Fall of Man, that it is also the primary effect seen and felt in the world today. The Enemy has not changed his tactics. His main goal is to place you in direct violation of the first commandment found in Deuteronomy 6:7, "You shall have no other gods before Me." If you have read the entire Bible, you will find a pattern that is repeated by mankind. It goes something like this: idolatry leads to servitude; servitude leads to repentance and cries for deliverance; God delivers and man makes grand promises; man breaks grand promises and falls into idolatry; idolatry leads to servitude.

For the reasons given here, you must be careful about desiring what this world offers you. The expected return on the investment the world will make in your life is perpetual slavery to idols. This statement should raise an important question in your mind. How are we to live in the world and yet resist its idolatrous influences? We are not called to draw distinctions between our postmodern culture and idolatry. To do away with idols is to reject a pluralistic, postmodern culture where idols draw their nutrition. In the words of D. A. Carson, "The New Testament writers did not readily distinguish the pluralism of the day from the idolatry of the day: the destruction of one was the destruction of the other."[4]

---

4. Carson, *The Gagging of God*, 497.

So what do we do with this dilemma? The apostle John provides an explanation.

Do Not Love the World: 1 John 2:15-17

It is no secret that once you spend time in the Johannine literature of the New Testament that you will encounter an abundance of teaching on the world. We have positive admonitions from the most well-known verse in the Bible, John 3:16, that "God so loved the world. . ." But it is a negative appeal which John gives in his later epistle that bears weight on our battle with idolatry. I would argue that the theological consequences expressed in Genesis 3 find their practical warnings in 1 John 2:15-17. Listen closely now to the words of the beloved disciple.

> Do not love the world nor the things in the world. If anyone loves the world, the love of the Father is not in him. For all that is in the world, the lust of the flesh and the lust of the eyes and the boastful pride of life, is not from the Father, but from the world. The world is passing away, and also its lusts; but the one who does the will of God lives forever.

I want to take some time here and break down for you the connections between this passage, the fall of man in Genesis 3, and the problem of idolatry in our postmodern culture. In order to do so, I need you to remember two important truths concerning biblical theology. First, it is not disingenuous to connect themes in the biblical narrative even though there are no direct Scriptural citations. So, the passage here in 1 John does not directly quote Genesis 3, but that does not mean they are not connected. Second, tracing biblical theology involves addressing meta-narrative realities. Postmodern thinkers are apprehensive of meta-narratives, but you cannot help but notice them as you read the Bible.

John begins this passage with a negative command. You, as a Christian, are not to love the world nor the things in the world.

The Biblical Description of a Fallen World

Someone might say, "Wait a minute. The world contains my family. I thought I was supposed to love them?" Here is where the professor in me starts to smile. The operative exegetical principle that you should apply whenever you read the Bible is, context determines meaning. Do you see the little word "for" in verse 16? In the Greek, as in English, it is a conjunction. What is a conjunction? Take a minute and Google *Schoolhouse Rock*. A conjunction is a word the links other words, phrases, or clauses together. The word "for" in this context is what we call an explanatory conjunction. In other words, John is explaining in verse 16 what he means by verse 15.

When John says, "Do not love the world," he means the things of the world, that is, the lust of the flesh and the lust of the eyes and the boastful pride of life. John is not saying that we cannot love our family, friends, or neighbors. It is ridiculous to think that he is teaching that we are not to love lost people in the world. Such an interpretation would be in direct violation of Jesus' own words. Keener rightly notes that when John speaks of the world, he does not mean "the entire created order, but rather humans who love the world."[5] The focus of John's teaching is on the things of the world that enslave humans.

Idols of our own creation are masters at forcing servitude upon us. The three descriptions of the things "in the world" given in this text are idols that find their origin in the actions of the very first man and woman. First, John warns us against the *lust of the flesh*. The latent desire present within Adam and Eve was awakened through the temptation offered by Satan. The desire of their flesh was to eat, only they were commanded by God that they could have anything they wanted to eat from any tree in the Garden except one. God did not place a limit on their satisfaction, but the boundaries of their satisfaction.

Our flesh craves things that are not profitable. One of my fleshly downfalls, and I have many, is ice cream. I love it and my desire for it is insatiable. I remember as a kid ordering a banana split from Dairy Queen and finishing it before we arrived back at our house less than a mile away. Even though my flesh craves

---

5. Keener, *The Gospel of John: A Commentary*, 395.

ice cream, it produces in me horrible results. I will spare you the details, but just ask my children about car rides with their slightly lactose intolerant father. Your flesh will always seek satisfaction without boundaries and for that reason it is an atrocious god. The desires your flesh produces on its own are the most difficult idols to destroy. If you do not believe me, then try and abolish the dessert table at the next Baptist potluck.

Next, John mentions *the lust of the eyes*. It is here we see a clear connection with the Edenic narrative. We are told in Genesis 3:6 that Eve, "saw that the tree was good for food, and that it was a delight to the eyes." The moment our eyes begin to lust after something, our actions become more difficult to control. Our eyes often reveal our desires and they are fairly accurate predictors of future behavior. God created Adam and Eve with sight, but so that they might see that the creation was good and full of God's glory. Genesis 2:9 says, "Out of the ground the Lord caused to grow every tree that is pleasing to the sight and good for food; the tree of life also in the midst of the garden, and the tree of the knowledge of good and evil."

The divine gift was warped into a vessel for idolatry. Yes, the tree of the knowledge of good and evil was turned into an idol by Adam and Eve. They saw it for something it was never intended. It became a means for them to replace the wisdom God was giving to them through direct revelation. Remember, at this point in history, God is speaking directly to and walking with humanity. Prayer is not a subjective experience for this couple, it is a face to face conversation. Adam and Eve allowed the allure of the tree that they were not supposed to eat from, clothed in the warped promise of Satan to take the place of the presence of God in their lives. Idols always try to take the place of God.

Your eyes, left unchecked, will always lead you down idolatrous paths. If you are skeptical of this truth, then read the words of Jesus in Matthew 5:27–30 regarding the eyes and the sin of adultery. He essentially says that looking at a woman in lust is the same as breaking the seventh commandment. Jesus goes on to say that if

The Biblical Description of a Fallen World

your eye causes you to stumble, then you should pluck it out and throw it from you. Why does he make this extreme statement? It is because Jesus knows the history of humanity and the eyes. He was present when the lust of the eyes turned his creation into an idol.

Psalm 101:3 says, "I will set no worthless thing before my eyes; I hate the work of those who fall away; it shall not fasten its grip on me." This royal psalm of King David underscores the importance of guarding our eyes against idols. The question which deserves asking of you is, are there worthless things that you are setting before your eyes? Have these things fastened a grip on you? I do not believe that David is talking about cutting the chord to your local cable TV box or cancelling your subscription to Netflix. He is saying, like the apostle John and within earshot of Genesis, that the lust of the eyes is a powerful idol.

Finally, John addresses *the boastful pride of life*. At the core of idolatry sits humanity's greatest enemy, pride. An argument could be made here that the sin of pride is what drove Adam and Eve to consume the divinely forbidden fruit. According to Wenham, the slight alterations that the serpent and the woman make to God's commands, "suggest that the woman has moved slightly away from God towards the serpent's attitude."[6] We know from Scripture that the serpentine sin was pride in believing he could be like God.

Pride is one of the foulest idols that exists in a broken world. Pride, more than any other idol in our postmodern culture, has consumed and destroyed numerous lives. The subtle lie of this idol is that you deserve to be recognized and applauded for who you are and what you have accomplished. Pride will always lead you to boast in yourself, even when what has been accomplished in your life is a direct result of God's sovereign action. Whenever I am tempted to think more highly of myself than I ought to think, I open the bottom drawer of my credenza in my office. It is there I find my Cracker Barrel employee of the year plaque along with numerous other awards. My students do not care that I was a great cook or waiter fifteen years ago. They need to see Jesus. By the way,

---

6. Wenham, *Genesis 1–15*, 73.

I have a chef's coat embroidered with the same accolade in the back of my closet at home.

Jesus warns us against pride when he asks in Matthew 16:26, "For what will it profit a man if he gains the whole world and forfeits his soul? Or what will a man give in exchange for his soul?" Listen my friend, the idol of pride will always whisper in your ear that the gains you have made in life are enough to barter with God for your soul. Pride will convince you that you are good enough to earn heaven and help God out with any potholes that need fixing along the way. The optimal teaching of the Bible is that you deny, not exalt yourself. You must be prepared to lose your life in order to find it securely in the arms of the Father. The idol pride pushes is antithetical to this truth.

Now that the connections are drawn between the Genesis account and the Apostle John's warnings against the things in this broken world, I want to bring to the table one of the elements of postmodernism for your further consideration. My goal here is to bring to bear the relationship between the grand narratives of Scripture and how they are reflected in our culture. The postmodern illusion of freedom that we learned about in chapter two is important for understanding how idolatry thrives in a broken world.

You may recall that a claim was made that the more our culture embraces radical egalitarianism, then the more we will experience a demand from the masses for an increased tolerance of immorality. The false idol of freedom opens a bottomless pit of immoral behavior from which a culture, apart from true repentance and revival, will not be able to escape. Once again, freedom is not the goal of your Christian life. Our postmodern culture will lead you to the feet of a false god that says it is perfectly acceptable to lust without boundaries and boast about it to all without any fear of consequences. This fact is why John's clarion call of warning fits not only in the first century, but in any century. It is timeless because it addresses a broken world, one that has been in existence since Adam and Eve sunk their teeth deeply into the fruit.

The Biblical Description of a Fallen World

A Charge for Endurance: 2 Corinthians 4:1–12

I realize that by this time in the chapter you are wondering if there really is any hope of faithfulness in a postmodern idolatrous culture apart from the return of Jesus. Maybe, but I would like to think the Bible gives us an answer. Not that I am against Jesus coming back. By all means, come quickly, please. The solution for surviving in a broken world saturated with idolatry is the New Testament's call for perseverance. There are many passages that speak to this idea, but few louder than 2 Corinthians 4.

Paul says in 2 Corinthians 4:4 that "the god of this world has blinded the minds of the unbelieving so that they might not see the light of the gospel of the glory of Christ, who is the image of God." It is probable that Paul has in mind here an allusion to the clay jar metaphor which arrives a few verses later in the context. So, the primary way that humanity sees the light of the gospel, even though Satan tries to keep them in the dark, is through Christians who persevere through suffering. We do not lose heart in a postmodern, idolatrous world because God is manifesting his truth through our mortal flesh.

The adversative refrain of 2 Corinthians 4:8–9 is a reminder for us to persevere in a broken world. By way of application, consider the encouragement of Paul. Yes, you will be afflicted in every way by idols, but they cannot crush you. Postmodernism is perplexing, but it must not lead to despair. Your rejection of idolatry may bring persecution into your life, but God has not forsaken you. There may come a day when our culture sees fit to strike you down, but be sure of this truth; it may claim your physical body, but you have an eternal weight of glory coming that is beyond all comparison. Your call as believers in the midst of a hostile culture is to stand your ground and say, "No, we will not bow down."

The main reason why God preserves and does not remove us from an idolatrous culture is so that we may bear witness to the truth of the gospel. It is so we might make known the living God, the One who is uncreated and eternal. I am talking about evangelism, a word that causes a majority of believers to shudder or comment that it is not their particular spiritual giftedness. I hate to burst another bubble, but you are commanded to be a verbal witness of the gospel whether you feel like it or not. I would argue that the more complacent you become with sharing the gospel, then the greater the probability will be that you will look more like the postmodern culture than you do Christ.

Stephanie's Evangelistic Perseverance

There are only a few people I have met in life that are more bold and straightforward about their faith in Jesus than my wife, Stephanie. It is not because she is the oldest of four children. Certainly, my seminary degrees did not seep into her sanctification like spiritual osmosis. Her confidence for the gospel is not because she attended a really great Bible study and was convicted of her need to change. No, her boldness is a present reality because she has tasted death.

Do not let anyone tell you that death is poetic and serene. It is scary and chaotic. Eleven years ago, Steph approached me at church on a Wednesday night to say that she was not feeling well. She asked if she could go home and rest. When I arrived home later that evening, I found her in bed suffering from what I thought was the flu. I was wrong. Throughout the night she began to get worse. To put it mildly, I was unsympathetic to her plight. I just wanted to sleep and even now I regret many things I said to her in the middle of the night. Sinners are ugly creatures and marriage has a way of exposing just how ugly we are. I am no exception.

The next morning I knew something was seriously wrong. The light of day revealed a paleness on her face that was scary. I made a decision to take her directly to the emergency room. To this day, I do not know why I did not call an ambulance. Instead, I pulled the car up to the middle of our yard and carried out my weakened bride, placing her in the passenger seat. We arrived at the hospital and they quickly admitted her. Later, the nurse told us that if I had called an ambulance they would have sent her away. We were to discover soon enough that this decision possibly spared her life.

The Biblical Description of a Fallen World

Not long after being assessed in the emergency room, the ER doctor decided Steph needed to stay for a while. The flu was at epidemic proportions and he felt that she would require some fluids because of dehydration. During her examination, she complained about pain in her shoulders because of passing out on the way back from the bathroom at our house. The physician ordered an X-ray just to make sure nothing was broken. In preparation for the test, the nurse asked the standard question, "Do you think you might be pregnant?" We actually laughed at the possibility, but then deferred to erring on the side of caution.

A little while passed and the nurse returned to let us know that indeed, the blood they had drawn returned a positive result for pregnancy. We laughed again and then talked about preparing for our fourth child. Because the hospital was so full with flu ridden patients they placed Steph in a temporary room. She remained somewhat stable even though her coloring was not getting better. I was scheduled for a meeting with some local ministers at the hospital that same morning and after encouraging me that she would be fine, I stepped out of the room for a few minutes. I was only in the meeting briefly before I was called back to my wife's side. I will never forget what the next few minutes would hold for her.

Allow me to offer a word of advice. If you ever enter a hospital room where doctors and nurses are running around frantically, something has gone terribly wrong. This scene was the one I met as I returned to Steph's room. My eyes immediately met my wife's and what I saw there was fear. Thankfully, my good friend Scott Brawner was there in the room with me. Scott, an Army Ranger and youth pastor at the time, kept me calm. Before I could reach the bedside a young female doctor stepped in front of me. She said very abruptly, "Mr. Turner, your wife has had an ectopic pregnancy. She is a lot of danger and we need to get her into surgery right away. Do not worry, I am going to take care of her."

For those of you who do not know medical terminology, an ectopic pregnancy is where the baby gets attached to the Fallopian tube and not the uterus. As the baby grows, the tube cannot contain the growth and it bursts, causing internal bleeding. It is often a silent killer. My wife had been losing blood for eighteen hours. Later we would learn that her hemoglobin count was measured at a 2 when normal is 12–14. When the doctor opened her up on the operating table she lost 3/5 of her blood supply. It is truly a miracle that she is still alive.

What happened next shocked me. I knelt by Steph's bed and she asked me, "Am I going to die?" How do you answer a question like that one? Before I could get an answer out, the young doctor began to give orders for Steph to be moved quickly into surgery. The room was buzzing, you could barely hear from all of the people bumping into each other as final preparations were made. That is when I heard the voice of my wife, strong and confident give a command. She simply said with authority, "Everyone, STOP!"

The ensuing seconds were jaw dropping. Everyone in the room turned to look at the critically ill young woman with the loud voice. Before anyone could begin moving again, Steph pointed a finger at the young, blonde doctor and said with clarity, "Are you the one who is going to operate on me?" The doctor nodded her head and began to speak, that is, until Steph interrupted her with these words, "You tell me right now," she continued with her finger pointed right at the doctor, "Are you a believer in Jesus Christ?" The young surgeon did manage to get the words "Yes I am," out of her mouth before Steph said in front of a stunned room, "Good, then give me your hands. I want to pray over you."

Nobody stopped Steph from leading us in prayer. The moment she finished they wheeled her out of the room into surgery. I collapsed into Scott's arms, weeping over the unknown outcome of the situation. God spared Stephanie's life and that boldness for the gospel she exhibited has not dimmed over the years. It has grown and blossomed into an incredible testimony of perseverance in a dark world. By the way, God did bless us with one more child. Her name is Clare, spelled in an unusual way. The doctor who saved Steph's life shares the same name with the same spelling. She was there to deliver Clare into the world.

The Biblical Description of a Fallen World

May I say that the same confidence displayed by my wife should be yours also? I do not mean that you have to literally end up moments from death on an operating table in order to be good at evangelism. I do mean to imply that the temporary nature of this broken world should lead you to confidently persevere for the sake of the gospel. Again, the primary reason God may not remove us from a pagan, idolatrous, postmodern culture is so that we might demonstrate great perseverance and display the light of Jesus. Imagine how much different the book of Daniel would be if he had chosen to acquiesce to culture. Do not be afraid of the pit of lions. God can shut their mouths.

Biblical Solutions and Application

The world is not going to fix itself or even make enough repairs to offer hope of a safe and secure life for you as a Christian. Unless something dramatically changes in our Western culture, idols will not only survive, but they will thrive and continue to exert more power over the lives of their blind worshippers. What, then, should you do in the midst of this broken, idolatrous culture? How can you stand firm even when most around you are oblivious of their slavery to these hollow gods?

First, you must hold tightly onto this truth, *you are a temporary resident in this world.* This world is not your home. You are not a citizen of the United States or any other country on the face of this earth. You are a citizen of heaven. Peter in his letter to the scattered believers reminds you that your inheritance is in heaven.[7] It is imperishable, undefiled, and will never fade away. It is in light of this objective reality that 1 Peter 2:11 reminds you as strangers and aliens "to abstain from fleshly lusts which wage war against the soul." Here is a piece of good news. Idols only have a temporary influence over your life.

Second, as a temporary resident, *you must persevere for the sake of the gospel.* Your resistance to the allure of idolatry is not so

---

7. See 1 Peter 1:3–4.

that you may gain patches to sew onto your sanctification vest. No, you are called to persevere in a postmodern culture so that your life is distinctively different from those around you. Hear the wisdom of 1 Peter 1:14 when he writes, "As obedient children do not be conformed to the former lusts which were yours in ignorance." Did you catch that command? You may resemble the culture where you live, but let me urge you to be a nonconformist.

Finally, *you must be a bold, verbal witness to the gospel.* The days are long gone where you can live a good, silent life and people will know that you are a Christian. I might actually argue that the Bible pushes you towards a different style of evangelism. In a postmodern culture, you need to speak the truth confidently, not arrogantly. You do not have to be offensive when sharing the gospel with your postmodern neighbors. Trust me, the gospel will do a fine job of offending people on its own. It is time for you to unashamedly refuse agreement and common ground with idols. A broken world deserves to see Christians who will not bow down or comprise their convictions.

7

Biblical Solutions for Living Faithfully in a Postmodern Context

Postmodern Redux

THROUGHOUT THIS BOOK I have used the term postmodern to mean a set of beliefs about knowledge, freedom, and language that are grounded in the rejection or modification of the modern notion of these ideas. With the –ism suffix added to the end of postmodern, I have implied that we are interacting with a firmly entrenched system that does not appear to be fading or even transforming into something new. It is a frightening worldview adopted ignorantly by the masses of our Western culture. More importantly, I have argued that postmodernism is a perfect breeding ground for the creation and worship of idols.

The modern idea of the worship of man, fueled by Enlightenment rationalism and skepticism has morphed into a more dangerous principle: individual communities within our cultures worshipping their own deconstructed, subjective realities. Tolerance will only last so long in such an environment before outright tribal warfare becomes the new normal. I am not a prophet. We are seeing it play out in the West right before our eyes. The hope we must pursue will never be found in the collective potential of humanity, but in the constant preaching of the gospel to every tribe and tongue.

Obviously, there is much more that could be said and will be said about postmodernism and idolatry. My goal here was to simply scratch the surface and raise awareness for those blinded by the culture we live in and interact with each day. Hopefully, we have done much more than just enlighten you, as along the way we uncovered some key biblical principles for living faithfully in this broken world. Idolatry is not a temptation that is going to retire and leave you alone once you reach a certain level of Christian maturity. It is an inescapable struggle, but one through which you can persevere.

The creation of an anemic intellectual culture is one of the main reasons why we see friends, neighbors, and family members easily submit to idols. As our culture continues to reject objective truth in favor of consumeristic, subjective experiences, then we will observe a rapid slide into immorality. I have consistently attempted to make this connection for you. Idolatry and immorality are not strangers; they always go hand-in-hand. We shun objective truth because we do not want to give up our idolatrous pleasures.

Another primary argument I raised for you was around the issue of freedom. The warning given earlier deserves an encore: freedom is a terrible god. As our postmodern culture continues to demand the enforcement of radical equality, Christians will be forced to relinquish objective stances in favor of the greater good of the human community. This reality may actually serve a Kingdom purpose as Christians will no longer be able to blend into the culture. We should already look different. The infection of postmodernism must be purged from the church once and for all through a return to biblical discipleship.

The language of postmodernism is a final, critical component for understanding its connections with idolatry. It is not surprising that the increase of subjective religious discourse has led down the

Biblical Solutions for Living Faithfully

path of confusion about the identity of God. Even now, evangelicals in the West are preparing a societal meeting because disputes have arisen on the nature of the Trinity. Arius is currently waking up in his grave and rubbing his eyes. As objective truth is locked away and tolerance is exalted, the way we speak about God will always be warped. Postmodern language games will only be overcome through adherence to the historical truth claims of Scripture.

Principles for Living Faithfully: A Biblical Review

The gospel is the answer for the person seeking to live faithfully in a postmodern culture filled with idols. I have tried in various different ways to point you towards not only believing this truth, but embracing it. Each chapter articulated for you several practical biblical principles that bear repeating and summarizing. I am always interested in the "So what?" question, mainly because I realize there are many out there who ask this question whenever biblical truth pierces their heart. They want to know: *so what am I supposed to do now?*

I am going to regurgitate for you these practical principles from the previous chapters, but in a slightly different form. My hope is to take these critical principles and answer for you the following question: *how might my life (in a postmodern, idolatrous culture) be different if I obeyed these principles?* This new formulation will hopefully produce two results. First, it will remind you of the importance of embracing timeless biblical truths. Second, it will not only help you visualize a way forward in this cultural battle, but it will also illuminate the benefits associated with following a more biblical model of discipleship.

Chapter one interacted with the postmodern web of knowledge. Three biblical solutions were stated for you: God is the source of all that can be or should be known, start lining up your beliefs with Scripture rather than how you feel, and recognize the boundaries of your knowledge and live with humility. Once you live within the proper perspective of who God is and what can be known about Him, the less chance there is of you building a god out of your own feelings. Here is what this could become in your life. You will grow in the knowledge of God's holiness and your utter dependency on Him. The people who are in your life will begin to depend on your wisdom and knowledge because it is biblical and stable, not emotional and erratic.

Chapter two discussed the postmodern illusion of freedom. I outlined for you that freedom is not the goal of your Christian life and that radical equality belongs in the context of the church, not the culture. How does this work out positively for you as a Christian in a postmodern, idolatrous culture? For one, you will begin to look more like a disciple of Jesus than a disciple of culture. Trust me, people are going to start paying attention as you place restrictions on your freedom. Additionally, you will become a more biblical church member. Participation in the church will be less about you and your personal preferences and more about embracing a biblical, corporate identity. In other words, your church may become healthier.

Chapter three addressed the postmodern game of language. I reminded you of three key principles: theology is not just for the seminarian, build your life on the truth claims of the Bible, and be open to new evangelistic strategies. So what difference should these things make in your daily Christian life? As you begin to love theology and as the truth claims of the Bible seep into your sanctification, you will begin to love the people trapped in postmodern idolatry. It is a very real possibility that God could use you to lead people out of idolatry and into the light of the gospel. Just imagine for a minute the person in your life who is the most spiritually lost. What if God used you to remove the scales from their eyes?

Chapter four established the biblical diagnosis of the human heart. The primary principle raised repeatedly in this chapter was the negative admonition against trusting your heart. There are many possible outcomes if you apply this truth to your life. The primary one I am thinking about right now is in the domain of your personal relationships. No one will deny that relationships (friends, family, and marriage) are messy. Why are your relationships such a mess? Because people are broken. We follow the false, idealized idol of Western relationships that are impossible to achieve. Here is what could happen for you: your relationships will become more transparent and real. As a result, you could find healing of old wounds where once you were doubtful about such a possibility.

Chapter five illuminated the biblical reality of spiritual warfare. I forced you to consider that spiritual warfare is real, it must be waged corporately, and that victory is achievable in the present. Idols in our postmodern culture are terrified of the Christian that has prepared his heart and mind for battle. I promise you, once you have tasted victory over the influence of idols in your life, you will refuse complacency and surrender. I believe you could see your fellow church members find victory as well and together lead a triumphal procession of worship for the King who has set you free. There is beauty at the end of these great cosmic struggles.

Chapter six narrated the biblical description of a fallen world. You learned that you are a temporary resident in this world, that you must persevere for the sake of the gospel, and that you must be a bold, verbal witness to the gospel. Let me ask a rhetorical question. Who does not like to finish well? I mentioned earlier my love for running. The one thing I have never done when running a race is walk across the finish line. I do not care how exhausted I am, when I see the crowds cheering me on, I find that extra burst of energy and I run across the line with confidence. Read Hebrews 12:1–2. These verses can be your testimony.

Postmodern idolatry is not going to surrender its position in our Western culture. The bad news is that your life will not get easier. The good news is that your life will not get any easier. The Bible never promises you an easy life. It promises that your life will bring glory to God. Many times that means you choosing faithfulness in the midst of a hostile culture. Remember, the narrative of the New Testament is suffering now and glory later. You can live faithfully in a postmodern, idolatrous context. The results could be astounding as you shun the hollow gods that are nothing but empty vessels making empty promises.

Hollow Gods

Postmodern Case Studies

I want to do something a little bit unexpected with you. In the hope that you will further reinforce the applications from this book, I am going to propose for your consideration three fictitious case studies. The stress here is on the word fictitious. These scenarios in no way resemble or reflect actual people or events in my experiences as a pastor and a professor. I just wanted to make that clear so that my friends and family who are reading this book resist the temptation to accuse me of embarrassing them.

You may use these case studies for personal reflection, in your Sunday School or small group study, or even as a family devotional. The goal is not for me to provide the answers for you. I have already done that for six chapters. Hopefully, these case studies will make you think and ponder how to respond to people who are confused in our postmodern culture. One caveat, each case study is about a situation in the church. The reason for this is simple. My firm conviction is that before we got to war against idolatry in the culture, it must be addressed with the people of God. So, if you are ready, let us dive into our first example.

A Postmodern Youth Group. As the volunteer leaders of your church's youth group, one of your students during a Wednesday night Bible study brings up the following topic. She tells the group that lately she has been having really strange dreams. One of her friends suggested to her that she start a dream journal in order to make sense of these experiences. Over the past few weeks, she has come to the belief that journaling about her dreams is a more important experience than reading her Bible or praying. After all, she says, "God may be trying to tell me something through these amazing experiences." Before you can speak, several of the other youth group members affirm her testimony and encourage her to continue in this vision quest.

Questions: How would you as a youth leader address this situation? What principles of postmodernism does this scenario reveal? What is the biblical response to her experiences? How might her experiences be idolatrous?

Biblical Solutions for Living Faithfully

A Postmodern Sunday School Member. During Sunday School, a fellow class member sits down next to you. He clearly reeks of alcohol. After class, you confront him in the hall and ask him directly about the smell. He does not act offended, instead, he brushes your concern aside and says, "Who are you to judge me? After all, I am not a deacon or an elder. I am free to drink. I really do not see the big deal." Later, you learn from a friend that he was at an office party the night before and hanging all over one of his female colleagues. During the church service, your eyes lock onto the man's wife who has a look on her face that clearly says, "Help me, please."

Questions: As a fellow church member, should you address this situation or just look the other way? If you confront the man, then what should you say? Should you try and talk to his wife? Is there a biblical solution to this dilemma?

A Postmodern Pastor. At lunch one day after church, your friend mentions to you his concerns that the pastor has been using improper language from the pulpit. In his view, the sermons are becoming less about the Bible and more about what is culturally cool and hip. You remark that you have not noticed, but that you will pay closer attention. After the smoke clears and your ears stop ringing from the praise and worship time, you open the church bulletin. Your eyes fix on the title of the sermon, "Let it Go: Tolerance is a Virtue." The pastor begins exegeting Disney's *Frozen* from a bar stool while never opening his Bible.

Questions: Do you pack your bags and leave the church? Do you encourage your friend to confront the pastor? Should you confront the pastor? Is there a solution in the Bible?

A Picture of Redemption on the Steps of a Tibetan Buddhist Temple

Some of the case studies just mentioned may not ever happen to you. I pray that they do not, but the reality is that given enough time you will see some pretty weird things happen in the life of the church. As my friend and worship pastor Bill Shiflett used to say,

"Everyone is sipping from the cup of weird." Sometimes, however, God will do something really weird in the midst of dark places that makes you sit back and say, 'Wow." In order to illustrate this point, let me take you back to the steps of the Tibetan Buddhist temple.

Prior to the trip where I was chased out of the temple by an angry monk, I sat on the same steps a broken man. It was my first trip to China and I had some very prideful, false expectations. Our team from Lenexa Baptist was charged with learning and strategizing how to reach an unreached people group with the gospel. From the moment I stepped off of the plane, God began to tear down my pride. You see, I thought that we were going to take China by storm. After all, the team was loaded with tons of missions experience and expertise.

The moment I knew my error was walking through the airport in Beijing. I quickly came to the realization that I was going to be unable to speak or communicate with anyone. My acumen at Mandarin Chinese at that point was nonexistent. I did not even know how to greet someone properly, let alone share about the atonement of Jesus Christ for our sins. As we journeyed across the country and into the Tibetan regions, my frustration grew and despair set into my heart. I wrote these words in my prayer journal, "They have not heard the truth. The task seems so overwhelming. Only God can do something here. We are helpless without Him." I do not know if you have ever been to this place spiritually, but it is not fun.

Six days into the trip, my weariness reached critical mass. I sat down on the steps of the temple and prayed, "God, what am I doing here? This place is so dark. Are you even at work in this land?" Through tears, I arrogantly assumed the worst of my surroundings. That is, until God showed that He was doing something and that yes, we are helpless without Him. I finished praying and began walking up the steps. On the way up, my eyes met with four young Chinese girls walking down from the temple. They smiled and walked up to me. One of them said in perfect English, "Hello, how are you? Are you an American?" I was so shocked that I barely got out an affirmative answer.

Biblical Solutions for Living Faithfully

Little did I know that God was about to teach me something big about Himself. We shared some small talk during which I discovered that these young ladies had just graduated from high school and were on their senior trip. I thought to myself, "How can I turn the conversation to the gospel?" I assumed they were in Shangri-la because it is one of the holiest cities in Tibetan Buddhism. I asked them point blank, "Did you enjoy seeing the temple? You must be Buddhists, right?" My heart was not prepared for what happened next. They looked at one another, then looked around to see if anyone else was listening. Confident that everyone else on the steps was oblivious, one of the girls answered and said, "No, we worship Jesus."

It was at that moment that God pulled back the curtain on my unbelieving heart and whispered clearly, "See, I am doing something here." My aim is to give you hope. If God is at work in an openly idolatrous culture in the Far East, then he is surely at work in our secretly idolatrous postmodern one in the West. Be prepared for your eyes to be opened. God will often show up and remind you that without Him you are helpless.

What if I told you that even though you reside in a Western culture that you can see the same things happen every single day of your life? The idols we have created are subtle. They are invisible masters. The problem of idolatry is not new. It will continue until Jesus returns. But be encouraged, the hollow gods of our postmodern culture are no match for the eternal, Living God.

Bibliography

Bookidis, Nancy and R. S. Stroud. *Demeter and Persephone at Corinth*. Princeton: The American School of Classical Studies at Athens, 1987.
Bork, Robert H. *Slouching Towards Gomorrah: Modern Liberalism and American Decline*. New York, NY: Regan Books, 2003.
Bricault, Laurent and Richard Veymiers. "Isis in Corinth: The Numismatic Evidence, City, Image, and Religion." In *Nile into Tiber: Egypt in the Roman World, Proceedings of the IIIrd International Conference of Isis Studies, Faculty of Archaeology, Leiden University, May 11-14, 2005*, edited by Lauren Bricault, Miguel John Versluys, and Paul G. P. Meyboom, 392–416. Leiden: Brill, 2007.
Carson, D. A. *The Gagging of God: Christianity Confronts Pluralism*. Grand Rapids, MI: Zondervan, 1996.
Hafeman, Scott J. "Paul's 'Jeremiah' Ministry in Reverse and the Reality of the New Covenant." In *Paul's Message and Ministry in Covenant Perspective*, 107–115. Eugene, OR: Cascade Books, 2015.
Horsely, G. H. R. *New Documents Illustrating Early Christianity: A Review of the Greek Inscriptions and Papyri Published in 1979*. Vol. 4. Marickville, N. S. W.: Southwood Press, 1987.
Keener, Craig S. *The Gospel of John: A Commentary*. Vol. 1. Peabody, MA: Hendrickson, 2003.
Lewis, C. S. *The Screwtape Letters*. New York, NY: Harper Collins, 1942.
———. *Mere Christianity*. New York, NY: Harper Collins, 1952.
Litfin, Duane. *Conceiving the Christian College*. Grand Rapids, MI: Eerdmans, 2004.
Moo, Douglas J. *The Epistle to the Romans*. Grand Rapids, MI: Eerdmans, 1996.
Phillips, D. Z. *Wittgenstein and Religion*. New York, NY: Palgrave Macmillian, 1993.
Proctor, Bruce. *A Definition and Critique of Postmodernism: Its Traits in the Emerging Church and Relevance to Romans 1:18-32*. Dallas, TX: Xulon Press, 2012.
Rainer, Thom S. and Jess W Rainer. *The Millenials: Connecting to America's Largest Generation*. Nashville, TN: Broadman & Holman, 2011.

Bibliography

Ross, Allen P. *Creation and Blessing: A Guide to the Study and Exposition of Genesis.* Grand Rapids, MI: Baker Books, 1998.

Savage, Timothy B. *Power through Weakness: Paul's Understanding of Ministry in 2 Corinthians.* Cambridge, UK: Cambridge University Press, 1996.

Thompson, J. A. *The Book of Jeremiah.* Grand Rapids, MI: Eerdmans, 1980.

Tozer, A. W. *The Knowledge of the Holy.* Chicago, IL: James Clark, 1965.

Waltke, Bruce K. and Cathi J. Fredricks. *Genesis: A Commentary.* Grand Rapids, MI: Zondervan, 2001.

Wenham, Gordon J. *Genesis 1–15.* Vol. 1. Waco, TX: Word Books, 1987.

www.ingramcontent.com/pod-product-compliance
Lightning Source LLC
Chambersburg PA
CBHW070459090426
42735CB00012B/2622